THE IDEA OF GOD

THE IDEA OF GOD

A Whiteheadian Critique
of St. Thomas Aquinas'
Concept of God

by

BURTON Z. COOPER

MARTINUS NIJHOFF / THE HAGUE / 1974

ISBN 90 247 1591 1

PRINTED IN BELGIUM

To
Jennifer (1960-65)
whose life was perfect in its beauty

TABLE OF CONTENTS

ACKNOWLEDGMENTS

In my study of Whitehead and of Process Theology, I have acquired a great intellectual debt to Daniel Day Williams, my teacher, adviser and friend at Union Theological Seminary in New York City. I am, also, grateful to him for his encouragement of my work.

I thank the many writers of books and articles on Whitehead and Aquinas; I am especially appreciative of the work of Charles Hartshorne. My thanks, also, to the publishers mentioned in the footnotes for permission to use quotations.

During the writing of this book, I received financial grants from the College of Wooster in Ohio, Mary Washington College in Virginia, and Louisville Presbyterian Theological Seminary. I should like to express my appreciation for the help these institutions gave me.

The book, itself, is a much revised version of a doctoral dissertation submitted at Union some years ago.

I am grateful for the good will of my wife, children and friends.

Louisville   Burton Cooper
August 1973

I would like to add a belated acknowledgement to the feminist movement in theology. Were I writing this book today, I would not, of course, refer to God simply in the masculine gender nor would I use the term "man" in a generic sense.

BC

LIST OF ABBREVIATIONS

The following abbreviations have been used in footnote references :

PATRISTICS

C. Ar.	— Contra Arius
C. Cels.	— Contra Celsum
De Inc.	— De Incarnacion
De Princ.	— De Principiis
De Trin.	— De Trinitate
Naz.	— Gregory of Nazianzen
Nyssa	— Gregory of Nyssa

ST. THOMAS AQUINAS

C. G.	— Summa Contra Gentiles
De Pot.	— De Potentia
De Ver.	— De Veritate
Summa	— Summa Theologica

WHITEHEAD

P. R.	— Process and Reality
S. M. W.	— Science and the Modern World

PREFACE

Thinking about God is historical thinking and that in two senses : the idea of God has a history, and those who think about God think through an historically formed mind. The task of the theologian, is not the attempt to move outside his historicity – such an attempt constitutes a fallacy and not a virtue – but to accept its implications and limitations. Methodologically this means that the theologian must point to the historical perspectives that underlie the idea of God in its development and, in his own constructive thought, must work self-consciously with an historical perspective informed by the psychological and cosmological understanding of his own time.

This book centers on that idea which traditionally has been associated with the very godness of God – the idea of divine absoluteness – and puts certain historical, logical, religious and, finally, cosmological questions to it. The roots of that idea lie in Greek thought, which entered Christian theology via the early church fathers; even so, there is much indication, particularly in Patristic trinitarian thought, that the Biblical heritage is pushing theological thinking towards a social or relative concept of divine being (ch. 1). The idea of divine absoluteness achieves full and systematic development in the thought of Thomas Aquinas, so that a close analysis of Thomas is highly revealing in terms of laying out the logical and theological problems that arise out of the notion of absoluteness (chs. 2-6). What is interesting is that Thomas' trinitarian theology, even more than Augustine's, suggests a social or relative mode of divine being. Neither one of these thinkers drew out the social implications of trinitarian thought, the present situation is that trinitarian thinking stands as a rich but untapped theological doctrine in search of an ontological alternative to absolutism (ch. 7).

There is, of course, every reason to believe that Thomas was sensitive to the tensions in his thought as well as aware of the fact that trinitarian theology strains against an ontology of the absolute; it is not a superior awareness on our part of internal difficulties in Thomas' thought that divides us from him. The real dividing point is an historical one - something has happened in our history. Modern science has so qualified our understanding of things that we can know, perhaps even must know, ourselves and our world in a new way. The fundamental principle which informs our re-knowing is stated by Gerhard Spiegler when he writes that

In an age when the principle of relativity has established itself in the foundations of both modern physical science and historical scholarship, it seems appropriate to at least entertain the thought that Christian theology will also have to forego its mooring in modes of thought entirely predicated on some form of substantive absolutist type of thinking.[1]

What this means is that it is now possible for theology to break loose from the compulsion of its Greek heritage to conceive God as absolute; it need no longer be "unthinkable" to conceive deity and relativity together. The final chapter of this book, informed as it is by Alfred North Whitehead's metaphysical vision of a genuine reciprocity between God and world, seeks to work out a view of deity which is appropriate to the modern experience of nature and to the religious experience of the redemptive power of God. The justification of this procedure must lie in its fruits, which I believe to be threefold : some of the most intractable logical, moral and religious problems which have historically beset orthodoxy can now be met; an ontology is established which is at one with the direction of Trinitarian theology; and Christian faith is rendered more intelligible to the culture of this age.

It is impossible to write about the reality of God these days without speaking to those theologians who deny that reality. My feelings here are similar to those of Herbert Richardson when he argues that the "death of God" movement signifies not the birth of a new direction for theology but the end of the old one.[2] Though I would want to

---

[1] Gerhard Spiegler, *The Eternal Covenant* (New York : Harper and Row, 1967), p. xv. Spiegler strangely fails to mention that under the influence of Alfred North Whitehead's philosophy Charles Hartshorne, Bernard Meland, Daniel Williams, Norman Pittenger and, more recently, Schubert Ogden and John Cobb have been working out a theology thoroughly grounded in the principle of relativity.

[2] Herbert Richardson, *Toward an American Theology* (New York : Harper and Row, 1967), ch. 1.

add that those of us revising the concept of God have concerns similar to those who reject the reality of God, it is still, I believe, too hasty to say that we must now know our world as a world without God. Much theological confusion might have been avoided if we had seen quickly enough that the modern experience of nature meant the beginning of a post-Hellenic age rather than the beginning of a post-Christian age. What will not do in our era is not the idea of God as such but the Hellenic idea of God, not the idea of divine power but the Hellenic idea of divine power. Similarly what will not do is the Hellenic idea of being, time, eternity, otherworldliness, etc. The reason for this is clear enough: the world view on which the interpretation of these concepts was based has collapsed.

The rejection of Hellenic ideas which are deeply embedded in the Christian view of God is bound to undermine traditional doctrines. Nevertheless, such a move is necessary if we are to speak now, out of our own culture and history, about the reality of God and the meaning of redemption.

CHAPTER I

THE TENSION IN PATRISTIC THEOLOGY

What I want to establish in this chapter is that, at the very beginning of Christian theology, Christian thought about God strained in two directions. We can call one of those directions Hellenic, and the other Trinitarian. The issue raised here can be put in the form of a question : is the ontology implicit in the doctrine of the Trinity compatible with the notion of divine absoluteness explicitly affirmed by the early church? The answer to this question involves unpacking the ontological implications of Trinitarian thought, but it is necessary first to open up some of the issues involved in the concept of the absolute. We can begin with Plato's thought and its influence upon the early church fathers.

Plato accepted the conclusion of Heracleitus and Protagoras that sense perception disclosed a world of change, flux and impermanence; consequently, this world of sense and perception contained no real (eternally valid) truths. Plato took this to mean that the only possibility for real knowledge must be in a mode of knowing other than one rooted in the senses. We all know the crux of his solution : eternal truths are arrived at conceptually, not perceptually. The outcome of this dichotomized epistemology is the theory of two worlds corresponding to the two different ways of knowing. One is a world of pure reality, immune to change; the other is a world of relative actuality, characterized by coming and passing away. One world is and never becomes; the other becomes and never is.

Being, for Plato, or if you will, reality, is transcendent to flux or process; what is real is what is permanent. In so far as any thing is, it participates in being (specifically as a copy); in so far as any thing is characterized by change, it is informed by non-being, and is ultimately threatened with the sheer negation of whatever reality it possesses. Thus, Plato understood change as a threat to being and, in developing this strand of Plato's thought Hellenic theism radically uprooted all dimension of change from the understanding of divine being.

The fathers accepted the negative Hellenic interpretation of change and they affirmed the concept of divine absoluteness because it had the virtue of excluding by definition all elements of change in the divine being. For example, the affirmation of the absoluteness of divine power means that change flows from God never towards him; similarly, the absoluteness of divine knowledge means that being derives from (God's) knowing so that no temporal act could alter or change the divine knowledge. Again, the absolute impassibility of deity rules out any possible change in the emotional tone of God's being, and the notion that God is absolutely " *a se*" forbids the possibility of an external agent effecting a change in deity. It is worth stressing that the fathers pre-supposed God's absoluteness in all aspects of his being with neither qualification nor exception. God, says Athenagoras, is "uncreated, eternal, impassible, incomprehensible, uncontainable"; [1] for Theophilus, God is "uncontainable... He is without being because He is uncreated, and He is unchangeable because He is immortal". [2] Methodius affirms deity as "impassible and unalterable" and concludes that the "act of creation involved no change in the being of God himself". [3] Clement says that God is "impassible, without anger, and without desire". [4]

There is no end to the multiplication of such texts, for they belong not only to the fathers but to the history of Christian thought. We tend to forego radical criticism of them as if they were axiomatic to all reflection upon God. Whether they are axiomatic or whether they belong to what Whitehead refers to as "the history of mistakes" which refines our knowledge depends upon the seriousness of the difficulties into which their implication lead us. What then do they imply?

They imply, to begin with, the transcendence of deity to the creation, the incomparable superiority of God to all creatures. With this of course there can be no quarrel, but it is the character of this incomparable superiority, namely its absoluteness, with which I am

[1] Supplication 10.1, quoted by G. L. Prestige, *God in Patristic Thought*, (London : S.P.C.K., 1952), p. 3.

[2] Ad Autol 1.3, quoted by G. L. Prestige, *ibid.*, p. 3.

[3] De Creatis 4.1, quoted by Prestige, *ibid.*, p. 7.

[4] Stromata 4.23, quoted by Prestige, *ibid.*, p. 7.

here concerned. Take, for example, the idea of divine pervasion which involved the assertion that God contains all things but is contained by none. In so far as this notion affirms the divine presence as supporting, sustaining, and guiding the world, it rightly guards the truth of God's immanence. Insofar as it affirms the otherness of God in relation to the world, it rightly protects the transcendence of God. But the doctrine involves more than this. Nemesius is typical in claiming that God's being "penetrates everything without obstacle, but is itself impenetrable".[5] That is, to be is to have divine being enter into one's own determination but God has being in such a way as to be invulnerable to other beings constituting a factor in his self-determination. In other words, God is here understood as the exception to ontological principles, for the fathers are asserting not simply the universality of divine influence, but the one-directionality of this influence : namely, God penetrates, but he is inpenetrable.

The Platonic ontology behind this assertion is apparent enough; Being, that which really is, simply is, and never becomes.

It is not necessary here to analyse every attribute of God as interpreted by the fathers in order to demonstrate their Platonic presuppositions. For the moment, let me confine the discussion to the eternality of God and his impassibility.

When the fathers ascribed eternality to God their intention was to point not simply to the divine everlastingness but to the radical otherness of God's mode of being. For example, in Book XI of *The Confessions*, Augustine contrasts the eternal order, which is motionless, unchangeable, and perfectly realized, with the temporal order, which is transient, dynamic, and incomplete. Therefore, to say that God is eternal is to exclude him from subjection to the metaphysical categories of the temporal order of existence. Thus, the metaphysical principles that categorize all being are understood as irrelevant to the being of God. All being is a being in time, God's being is absolutely outside of time. God's timelessness means not only that God endures through all time but that all time is simultaneously present to God. The Platonic cosmology is transparent here; reality, or Being, does not admit of succession so that no aspect of God can be in time.

The doctrine of divine impassibility proved a particularly troublesome one for the fathers partly because it had to be maintained

---

[5] *The Nature of Man* 3, quoted by Prestige, *ibid.*, p. 32.

alongside the Old Testament picture of a wrathful, angry, repentant, merciful God, but mainly, and this is surely the truth that Sabellius laid hold of, because the very thrust of the revelation in Jesus Christ was that God saves the world by suffering in and with the world. The apparent Biblical attribution of suffering to incarnate deity was understood by the fathers as a Christological problem and it was met there by attributing the suffering of Christ to the human nature. The Biblical language which suggested the possibility of God the Father was explained away by allegorical exegesis. Thus, Clement of Alexandria urges that reverence alone requires that an allegorical meaning be extracted from such language. He holds that the possibility of mental variation is forbidden in divine being, and that therefore it is inadmissable to ascribe to God such passions or emotions as joy, pity, or grief; God is "without anger and without desire".[6] Clement offers two reasons to account for the "inadmissable" Biblical picture. First, the prophets adopted such language as a saving concession to the weakness of human understanding. Second, men are so enveloped by mortal concerns that they form suppositions of God similar to their own experiences.

What must be noted here is not so much Clement's discrediting the religious understanding and theological maturity of the Hebrew people, but that he never considers the possibility that the Biblical dramatic language about God might be implying an ontology at variance with the Platonic one. The reason for this is that the ontological presuppositions which are being brought to the Biblical texts serve to interpret the meaning of the text in such a way as to rule out the possibility of any qualification on the ontological level. For example, Clement cannot admit passibility into deity because he assumes, as do all the orthodox fathers, that God possesses a permanent, changeless mode of being. Cyril of Alexandria holds that "immutability exists in God by virtue of his nature",[7] and Alexander, Bishop of Alexandria, affirms the Father to be "immutable and invariable in his being, and always in the same identical mode of existence, admitting neither progress nor diminution".[8] To admit the suffering of God is to undermine the notion of divine absoluteness,

---

[6] Stromata 4.23, quoted by Prestige, *ibid.*, p. 8.
[7] St. Jn. 305C, quoted by Prestige, *ibid.*, p. 14.
[8] Ap Theodoret h.e. 1.4.46, quoted by Prestige, *ibid.*, pp. 12ff.

and this the fathers refused to do. Again, the Hellenic metaphysic is patent, and once again, but perhaps more forcefully here, we must ask whether such an ontology is adequate to the Biblical picture of God.

The sum of this analysis is that the Patristic doctrine of the divine perfections presupposes throughout a concept of being expressly forbidding the entrance of a dynamic, open, process aspect into deity. Perfect being in Patristic thought signifies full realization of being so that God's being is understood as ontologically independent and invulnerable to all that is thrown up by the ongoingness of the world. In such a view, the world is neither necessary for the perfection of God's existence, nor does its existence add a whit to the divine being. And this is necessarily so by the logic of absolutism. God's being, according to Bishop Alexander, admits neither progress nor diminution.

The point is not, of course, that the fathers believed God to be inactive, indifferent or uninterested in the happenings of the world. The fathers clearly grasped that the heart of the Biblical revelation was God's love for the world. The question is, what does it mean, ontologically, to affirm that God acts in history or that God is love. If love means the vulnerability of one being to the suffering of another, if it entails the risk of openness, the possibility of loss, and the hope of value, then Patristic thought never fully developed an ontology of love. For the fathers, God's will is determined from all time for all time sheerly from within; God's knowledge is of all time, the experiences of the world can add nothing to it. Thus, all elements of vulnerability, risk and novelty are removed as possible aspects of the divine mode of being. God's being is essentially an unrelated being. He is the same before and after the creation. Though God is not indifferent to the world, the happenings of the world make no difference to his being.

I have said that this notion of God's absoluteness finds its roots not in the Biblical witness to God but in a particular historical ontology. What I would like to argue now is that when orthodoxy turned to the task of working out an aspect of the idea of God peculiar to Biblical faith, namely the Trinitarian dogma, the ontology implied by that dogma turns out to be quite at variance with the Hellenic ontology underlying the doctrine of the divine perfections.

The occasion for the Christian doctrine of the Trinity was the theological necessity to encompass an historical personage and redeemer within deity.[9] It was informed by a soteriological conviction which ultimately insisted on the full divinity of one who was distinct from God the Father. The theological affirmation of the Son's full equality with the Father was a relatively late development. Tertullian allows a time when the Son was not. Origen's concept of the eternal begetting of the Son overcomes this temporal subordination, but other significant strains of subordination remain in Origen's thought. The Son, Origen writes, is a "secondary God",[10] that is, his deity is derivative, he is not himself the source and origin of his being, he comes into being out of the will of the Father.[11] The Son eternally issues from the Father as brightness from light, rays from the sun, a stream from water, a fountain from its source. The Son is the image of the Father's goodness, an effulgence of the divine glory, a faithful mirror of God. In the strictest sense, for Origen, the Father, as the ultimate ground of deity, alone possesses the fullness of unoriginate deity. The Son's goodness and truth is not absolute (unoriginate) goodness and truth, but a reflection, a mirror, an image of the Father's goodness and truth. But subordinationism cuts even deeper than this in Origin's thought; the mystery of divine being, the ineffability of God which marks God as very God is lodged in the Father alone. Thus, in discussing the depth of the mysteriousness of God, Origen remarks that full knowledge of God evades all created beings other than Christ and the Holy Spirit. It is the knowledge or reflection of the divine mystery, not the mystery itself, which belongs to the Son.

Now, what is at issue in Origen's trinitarian thought? First of all, the Son is neither temporally, nor substantially subordinate to the Father. The begetting of the Son is not an event in time, but it represents an eternally continuous process within the eternal being of God. There is no division of substance in this continuous process through which the Son issues forth from the Father; Father and

---

[9] Tillich argues that the need to reconcile the ultimacy of God with the concrete experience of him forces all monotheistic faiths, implicitly or explicitly, to deal with the "Trinitarian" problem. In this sense, Trinitarian thinking belongs not simply to the history of religions but to the philosophy of religion. Cf. Tillich, *Systematic Theology*, vol. i, pp. 228-229.

[10] Origen, *Contra Celsum*, E. T., Henry Chadwick, (Cambridge : Cambridge University Press, 1953), 2.64.

[11] Origen, *De Principiis*, E. T., G. W. Butterworth, (London : S.P.C.K., 1936), 4.4.1.

Son are the same substance.[12] Where the difficulty arises, where the second term of the Trinity is subordinated to the first, lies precisely on that line where the absolute unity, independence, and self-sufficiency of the Godhead crosses over into the relations of the deity with the world. That is, subordination comes in at the point where Origen seeks the solution to the problem of the one and the many : namely, how one moves from absolute unity and completeness of being to the multiplicity of the world. God as the perfect One, where perfection is Platonically understood as absolutely independent, fully realized being, is sufficient unto himself. On the other hand, the Biblical understanding of God as love, power, and goodness requires that God have objects on which to exercise his love, power, and goodness. In this light, the eternal begetting of the Son is seen as the attempt to mediate between God in his aseity and God in his relations. What God in his primary mode of being, as absolute independence, cannot be, God in his secondary mode of being, as related activity, can be. The Son is the agent of the Father in the creation, for all things come to be through the Son. Nevertheless this relational aspect of God lacks the fullness of deity. The Son is not the divine glory, but the image of that glory; not absolute goodness, but the mirror of goodness; not absolutely God, but derivatively God. Underlying this kind of analysis of deity is, of course, the Hellenic ontology. The godness of God lies in his oneness, absoluteness and beyondness; activity in the world of flux constitutes a threat to the deity of God, for it involves God in dynamic and therefore changing relations. The Son then must be understood as a secondary God, for it is only when we look beyond him that we find that form of being which is beyond relations and change.

Dr. Cyril Richardson, in his book *The Doctrine of the Trinity* [13] argues that Origen's thought is here covering up a problem universal to orthodox Trinitarian thought; namely, how the absolute can beget a mediator to the world when by its nature it is complete and, therefore, can have nothing "left over" for such a process. Richardson uncovers not only the logical inconsistency of such a concept as eternal begetting, he also holds that any attempt to relate God in his beyondness to God in his relations necessarily fails. The result

[12] De Princ. 4.4.1.
[13] Cyril Richardson, *The Doctrine of the Trinity*, (Nashville Tennessee : Abingdon Press, 1958), p. 59.

ot deriving one from the other, by the very nature of the terms, makes God in his capacity for relations an inferior God; it robs him of his absoluteness. Therefore Richardson argues that the godness of God must be understood as a paradox. God's being is both beyond relations and in relations, and neither way must be thought of as primary or prior to the other. Furthermore, Richardson rejects any attempt to remove this paradox : "In our need to do justice both to God's absolute transcendence and to his being in relations... we have reached the confines of human thought".[14]

Perhaps so. My argument is, however, that the sucessors to Origen, in seeking to root out subordinationist elements from Trinitarian thought, implicitly – perhaps "unconsciously" is a better term – rejected an absolutist conception of God. It is to the ontology implicit in Trinitarian doctrine, an ontology which the tradition has never drawn out, that I wish now to bring to your attention.

The theological task of the early church in coming to an orthodox doctrine of the Trinity was threefold : to guard the divine unity, to distinguish three "subsistences" within that oneness, and to protect the equality of the three "subsistences". This was a necessary task because, as Athanasius argued, the security of redemption through Jesus Christ is threatened unless the redeemer is fully divine. That is, Christian faith and experience demands the fullness of God incarnate. Athanasius' insistence on theologically (ontologically) protecting the reality of redemption in and through Jesus Christ simply overrides all Platonic hesitations in involving "ultimate deity" in the world. It is an absurdity, he holds, to suppose that the Father needs an intermediary in his relations to the world.[15] By consistently maintaining this conviction throughout, Athanasius attempts to rid Trinitarian thought of all elements of subordinationism.

The issue of the equality of the Son with the Father involves the eternity of the Son, his mode of generation, and his essence. Anthanasius holds that sonship implies succession only according to the human pattern, but not to the divine.[16] The rigorous use of logic requires that if God is understood as eternally Father, the Son must be understood as eternally Son. Further, the Son as the Father's

---

[14] *Ibid.*, p. 59.

[15] Athanasius, Contra Arius, *The Nicene and Post Nicene Fathers*, Second Series, Vol. IV, (New York : Charles Scribner's Sons, 1891), I, 2.24-26; 2.29.

[16] C. Ar., 123.

wisdom is necessarily eternal for it would be absurd to impute to God a time when he was without reason.[17]

The term *homoousios*, of the same stuff or essence, now serves to secure the essential or substantial equality of the Son with the Father. That is, Athanasius understands by *homoousios* an identity of essence. The Son, he writes, is "an offspring proper to the Father's essence... existing one in essence with the Father... The Godhead of the Father is the same as the Son's".[18] Rigorously logical to the end, Athanasius does not hesitate to draw the necessary outcome of his analysis. What is said of the Father, he holds, namely that He "is eternal, immortal, powerful, light, King, Sovereign, Lord, Creator and Maker... must be in the Image".[19] Similarly, he argues that if the Father is unoriginate or underived, then the Image or Mirror of the Father is necessarily unoriginate or underived (*agenetos*). Athanasius' attempt to deal with subordinationism here occasionally borders on mere semanticism. Thus, he urges us not to speak of the Son as derived, made, or created but as generated or begotten (*gennema*).[20] Where he moves beyond Origen is in the argument that to say God eternally begets is identical with saying that God is participation, or as Athanasius phrases it, is "entirely participated".[21] Anthanasius is apparently moving towards an emphasis on the oneness of the concretely acting God, though, of course, he never states that it is the Father who becomes incarnate as well as the Son.

The Son is distinguished from the Father as his agent in creation and redemption,[22] and as the revealer of the Father.[23] The meaning of the distinction is not Origen's, for the function of the Son, here, is not that of mediating the Father's absolute unity to the multiplicity of creation. Athanasius expressly condemns those who "assert that the creation is independent of the Father",[24] and he insists that there is no "artificer of all things other than the Father of our Lord

---

[17] C. Ar., I 14; 20.25.

[18] C. Ar., I 61.

[19] C. Ar., I 21.

[20] C. Ar. I 31.

[21] C. Ar., I 16.

[22] Anthanasius, "De Incarnacion" in Edward Hardie, ed., *Christology of the Later Fathers*, (Vol. III of the Library of Christian Classics, Philadelphia : Westminster Press, 1954), p. 265.

[23] De Inc. 31, 42.

[24] De Inc. 2.

Jesus Christ".[25] Athanasius' thought is that the Father creates through the Son, and this refers not to the Father's remoteness but to his immanence in the creation through the Son. Thus, Harnack is quite correct in his judgement that Athanasius understands "God as creator in the directest way". God's actions are all of a piece : when he acts, it is the Father acting through the Son; when he beholds himself, it is the Father beholding himself through the Son as His Image. In a word, the Son is "the expression of the Father's person".[26]

Thus, the shape of Athanasius' Trinitarian thought allows him to protect the unity of God. In formally ridding the term "Image" of its subordinationist connotations (as present in Origin where the Son's goodness is derived goodness), he has come to think of the Son not as a sphere of consciousness distinct from the Father, but as the divine self-consciousness itself. The Father as the source of the Son means for Athanasius that the Son is the expression of the Father, through whom the Father is apprehended.[27] The duality is still there in so far as the expression is not the expresser. Nevertheless, it is a kind of duality which implies the most intensive unity. Thus, we can say that in protecting the very Godhead of the redeemer, Athanasius has so radically involved the Father in the activity of the Son as to implicitly undermine an ontology which asserts a mode of divine being beyond relations with the world.

There is, of course, no question that the Cappadocians, in stressing the distinctions in deity, redressed the balance in Trinitarian thought. What I want to argue, however, is that this shift does not indicate a re-instatement of the Hellenic concern to mediate God's beyondness; rather it is an attempt to provide an ontological base for the Biblical witness to a "heavenly Father" and incarnate Logos.

The problem facing the Cappadocians was to reconcile the oneness of divine being with the plurality of deity suggested by the confessional language of Christian faith. The Cappadocians arrived at the formula which was later to receive Athanasius' somewhat reluctant approval; namely, one *ousia* (essence) in three *hypostases* (persons).

As finally made clear, *ousia* is to be understood as defined by Aristotle in the primary sense : namely, not generic essence but the concrete reality of an individual. That is, *ousia* does not refer to

---

[25] De Inc. 2.
[26] C. Ar. I 9.
[27] C. Ar. I 12.

the distinction between genus and species, for this would lead directly to polytheism, but to the particular substance of the concrete individual. Thus, Basil's polytheistic analogy of *ousia* to *hypostasis*, as mankind to men, is corrected by Gregory of Nyssa. Nyssa argues that "only those things are enumerated by addition which are seen to be individually circumscribed"; circumscription, referring to size, place, form and color, belongs to material things alone. God transcends these things and is therefore beyond circumscription. "What is not circumscribed", he concludes, "cannot be numbered".[28] Understood in this (analogical) way, numerical distinctions in the deity are not inconsonant with a monotheistic conception of God. Further underlining the unity of the three persons, Gregory of Nazianzen holds that within the divine monarchy there is "an identity of motion and a convergence of elements".[29] Thus the unity of deity is grounded in the unity of operation so that pluralism of action is forbidden.[30] There are not three separate actions, Nyssa writes, "but whatever occurs... occurs through the three persons".[31] Every divine action begins with the Father, proceeds through the Son and is completed by the Holy Spirit, but "no activity is distinguished among the persons as if it were brought to completion individually by each of them or separately apart from their joint supervision".[32] For the Cappadocians, then, there is a unity and singularity of all divine motion, operation and energy. The Father is God and the Son is God, but, Nyssa can argue, God is one because in the Godhead there can be discerned no difference of nature or operation. Similarly for Basil, that which "belongs to the Father is seen in the Son, and every thing that belongs to the Son belongs also to the Father, for the Son abides whole in the Father, and possesses the Father whole in himself".[33]

The doctrine of coinherence which provides the ontological ground for these assertions understands the Father and Son as receptive

[28] Gregory of Nyssa, "On Not Three Gods," in Edward Hardie, ed., *Christology of the Later Fathers*, (Vol. III of the Library of Christian Classics, Philadelphia : Westminster Press, 1954), p. 265.

[29] Gregory of Nazianzen, "The Theological Orations" in Edward Hardie ed., *Christology of the Later Fathers*, p. 161.

[30] Nyssa, *op. cit.*, p. 264.

[31] *Ibid.*, p. 262.

[32] *Ibid.*, p. 263.

[33] Basil, Epistles, *The Nicene and Post Nicene Fathers*, Second Series, (Vol. VIII, New York : Charles Scribner's Sons, 1893), Epist. 38.9.

and permeative of one another. Identical in extension, Father and Son contain one another in a mutual enveloping, or a mutual inter-penetrating, as "perfume in the atmosphere". By affirming the coinherence of the persons, the Cappadocians sought to affirm the unity of the divine operations and the undifferentiated quality of the divine essence. The distinctions, which refer not to the essence, are made in regard to the idea of causality. "One is the cause, the other depends on the cause" and the third "is derived from what immediately depends on the first cause".[34] That is, the individual characteristics or particularities consist in being unbegotten or ingenerate (*agennetos*), begotten or generated (*genetos*) and processive. "Begotten" and "unbegotten" refer not to the essence of God [35] but to "the relation in which the Father stands to the Son and the Son to the Father".[36] That is, they represent not elements in being but merely modes in which the divine substance is transmitted and presented. In each *hypostasis* one and the same divine being is pre-sented in distinct objective and permanent expression.

Thus, Nyssa remarks that "to say that something exists (with or) without generation explains the mode of its existence".[37] The names of the Triad, then, do not represent *ousia*, essence, but the modes of relations within the divine being. These relations have no temporal reference but express eternal processes continually operative within deity. In Nazianzen's telling phrase, "to be begotten... is concurrent with to be",[38] motion itself is eternal in deity.[39] Here the Biblical, dynamic, active God is given his ontological ground.

The Son as the Image of the Father suggested for Athanasius the Father beholding himself in the Son. It was essentially an assertion of unity rather than distinction; the idea being that the Son is the self-consciousness of the Father. Modifying this, the Cappadocians held that each hypostasis is a sphere of conscious being. Thus, Nazi-anzen speaks of a "union of mind",[40] Nyssa of a "joint supervision" [41] and of the divine will present in each *hypostasis*.[42] In other words,

[34] Nyssa, *op. cit.*, p. 269.
[35] Naz., *op. cit.*, pp. 166 ff.
[36] *Ibid.*, p. 171.
[37] Nyssa, *op. cit.*, p. 267.
[38] Naz., *op. cit.*, p. 165.
[39] *Ibid.*, pp. 161, 165.
[40] *Ibid.*, p. 161.
[41] Nyssa, *op. cit.*, p. 263.
[42] *Ibid.*, p. 264.

the Trinitarian distinctions function to provide the ontological ground for those scriptural texts witnessing to the distinct conscious-ness of Father and Son, as well as to the distinctness of the Holy Spirit.

The Cappadocians were successful in meeting the formal require-ments of their task; their formulation safeguards the equality of the three modes of being and provides for the concrete, individual, and empirical objectivity of each person without destroying the ontolo-gical unity of deity (*ousia* signifying the concrete metaphysical reality identical in each *hypostasis*).

Now, the crux of the Cappadocian resolution of plurality in unity is of course, the doctrine of coinherence, the mutual interpenetration of the three persons issuing in a community of motion, operation, and energy. From a Platonic point of view the ontological implications of this doctrine are revolutionary. Nevertheless, before drawing out these implication I wish to set forth Augustine's related doctrine of appropriations. Here, also, a concept developed to meet the Trini-tarian problem points away from an ontology of the absolute.

Paralleling Cappadocian thought, Augustine affirms the insepara-bility of the three persons in the divine unity of their operations. Thus he writes, "whether we hear, show us the Son; or whether we hear, show us the Father, it is even all one, since neither can be manifested without the other".[43] Augustine's thought here is that given the coin-herence of the persons any given manifestation is properly the mani-festation of the whole Trinity. The doctrine of coinherence, however, left him without a firm principle by which to determine the Person manifested. Thus, in dealing with the theophany at Mt. Sinai, Au-gustine discovers that it is not plain "whether God the Trinity spoke, or the Father, or the Son, or the Holy Spirit severally".[44] He reaches a similarly inconclusive end respecting the appearances in the pillar of cloud and of fire [45] and in the vision of Abraham.[46]

Two things must be noted : first, the affirmation of the Father's appearance, and indeed of the whole Trinity, indicates abandonment of the absolute-related distinctions. Second, Augustine has obliterated the distinct roles of the three persons; eg. as creator, redeemer,

---

[43] Augustine De Trin., *The Nicene and Post Nicene Fathers*, First Series, Vol. III, 1887, 1.8.17.

[44] De Trin., 2.15.26.

[45] De Trin., 2.14.24.

[46] De Trin., 2.10.19.

sanctifier, or as source, agent, completer. Significantly enough, Augustine never saw the need to reconcile this obliteration of roles with his doctrine of the divine attributes which requires an aspect of God unrelated to and absolutely independent of the world process. This tension in his thought, as in the thought of the next great Trinitarian thinker, Thomas Aquinas, simply remains unresolved and almost unnoticed.

What Augustine turns to is the search for a working principle which, given the indivisibility of the divine action, would function to remind the church that God is triune. The principle he comes up with is that of the appropriation of any given divine event to that person to whom it appears most fitting by virtue of his internal relation within the deity. In other words, given the distinctions of relation within the Trinity (the Father as the beginning of the Godhead, the Son as issuing forth ,and the Holy Spirit as the unifying principle of Father and Son), Augustine argues that there is a kind of pedagogical justification in correlating the character of the manifestation with the character of the internal Trinitarian distinction. For example, the whole Trinity is involved in the creation,[47] the Incarnation,[48] and the baptism of Jesus,[49] but we appropriate these divine events to the persons severally because each event suggests a quality peculiar to one of the persons in the internal relations of deity. "In order to intimate the Trinity", Augustine writes, "some things are separately affirmed... the Persons being each severally named; and yet are not to be understood as though the other persons were excluded on account of the unity of the same Trinity".[50] Note here that Augustine has specifically disavowed any literal correlation between the external operation of deity and the internal distinctions (the economic Trinity is not rooted in the immanent Trinity). In the divine ontology, the Father is absolute source of deity, but in his relations to the world the Father loses his sheerly absolute character. He is absolute in some respects, namely as the ultimate source of all being, but he is relative in others. Further, by the doctrine of coinherence, whatever role the Father plays in any event is shared by both the Son and Holy Spirit. In other words, the Trinity as a whole is absolute in some respects and relative in others. Clearly,

[47] De Trin., 5.13.14.
[48] De Trin., 2.3.9.
[49] De Trin., 4.21.30.
[50] De Trin., 1.9.19.

what has happened in the history of Trinitarian thought from Athanasius to Augustine is that the distinction between the absolute and
related characteristics of God has shifted from an explicit distinction
between Father and son to an implicit distinction in the one Godhead.
But not only were the implications of this shift for the doctrine of
God never drawn out, but the shift itself was never consciously
acknowledged, so that certain problems continued to unsettle the
doctrine of the Trinity. For example, while the doctrine of appropriations is not intended to yield any knowledge of God, but functions
merely to remind us of the revealed truth that the One God is three,
it breaks down at the point of the Incarnation. The logic of the
"appropriations" would have Father, Son, and Holy Spirit incarnate,
with the manifestations appropriated to the Son by virtue of his
derived relationship. Yet Augustine argues that scripture forbids
our thinking of the Father as incarnate because "we nowhere read
that He is sent",[51] it is written only that the Son is sent. Seeking
ontological ground for the Incarnation of the Son alone, Augustine
holds that the Son is sent by the Father "not because the one is
greater, the other less... but because the one begetter, the other
begotten, the Son from the Father, not the Father from the Son".[52]
Further, the Father could not be said to be sent because "He has
no one of whom to be, or from whom to proceed".[53] Clearly, Augustine is here grounding an external divine operation in the internal
relations of the deity. The Son becomes incarnate because he is
begotten, the Father cannot become incarnate because he is unoriginate source.

Now both the doctrines of Appropriations and Coinherence, in
order to protect the indivisibility of the divine essence, expressly
deny that the internal distinctions of deity bear any direct correlation
to God's worldly activity. And though Augustine has implicitly
contradicted his own thought on this matter in seeking the ground
for the incarnation of the Son alone, he still insists that "the Son
is not properly said to have been sent in that He is begotten of the
Father".[54]

---

[51] De Trin., 2.5-8.

[52] De Trin., 4.2.27.

[53] De Trin., 4.20.28.

[54] De Trin. 4.20.28. The continuation of the quotation provides the proper
meaning of sent : "either in that the Word made flesh appeared to the world ...
or in that from time to time, He is perceived by the mind of each".

Dr. Richardson locates the source of this confusion in the fact that the sending of the Son is based on precisely the ontological distinction which the doctrines of Appropriations and Coinherence have abandoned : namely, the Father as absolute source of all, the Son as the principle by which that source is mediated to the world. "Is the Son not precisely sent", Dr. Richardson asks, "because He is derived from the Absolute and thus able to come into relations with the world in a way the Father cannot"?[55] Yes and no? More is involved here than either correcting an inconsistency in Augustine's thought or dropping off the third Person from the ontology of the Trinity.

First of all, Augustine's explicit ground for the formulation of the sending of the Son lies in his understanding of the authority of the Bible as the revealed word of God. Thus, he writes that "if thou, O God, wert Thyself the Father and wert thyself the Son... we should not read in the book of Truth, 'God sent his Son' ".[56] Secondly, and more significant, Dr. Richardson does not give sufficient weight to the fact that the history of Patristic Trinitarian thought witnesses to a continual cutting away at the old, explicit absolute-related distinctions. Thus, the mediating logos of philosophic thought is deliberately absent from Athanasius' theology, where the whole Trinity is related to the world in the most direct way, And as the discussion on the Cappadocians and Augustine indicates, the direction of Trinitarian thought moves more and more in line with the Biblical concept of an active, dynamic God wholly related to the world.

Yet this criticism does not wholly meet Dr. Richardson's argument. For he is dealing with both a metaphysical problem and a soteriological issue. This problem is recognized in Origen's thought, but it is inadequately dealt with there. For Origen, the Father, as alone unoriginate and absolute, alone transcends mind and being itself. He is sheer beyondness, He is One! Yet, "His essence being his attributes", his perfect love, goodness and power necessitate the creation from eternity. The world is brought into being through the mediation of the eternally begotten Son. Where Origen erred, Richardson argues, is in thinking of God in his capacity for relations as inferior to God in his absolute independence. The religious soterio-

---

[55] Richardson, *The Doctrine of the Trinity*, (Nashville, Tenn. : Abingdon Press, 1958), p. 78.
[56] De Trin. 15.28.51.

logical consciousness requires the equality of both modes of being. God must have eternally overcome non-being and yet still be involved with non-being, or redemption cannot be secured. That is, without the former, redemption is uncertain, without the latter, a Redeemer is impossible.

Now in their Trinitarian thought neither the Cappadocians nor Augustine have allowed room for this metaphysical-soteriological function of plurality. The distinctions they formulated are meaningful only in regard to the internal relations of deity. In regard to the question of God's relations to the world, the distinctions, upon close analysis, vanish. The whole Trinity takes upon itself the risks of involvement in the world.

This is precisely where Dr. Richardson finds the crux of the problem. Consider the Cappadocian distinctions of the Father as the beginning of all divine activity, the Son as actualizing the activity, and the Holy Spirit as completing it. There is no reason, Richardson argues, why the actualizer cannot complete his own activity and why he should be subsistently differentiated from the source. Or consider the faulty logic in arguing that these distinctions arise from the Christian experience of (1) God (the Father) as creator and law giver, (2) man in communion with God (the Son), and (3) man wholly controlled by God (the Holy Spirit).[57] There is no reason to assume that three (or thirty-three) distinct religious experiences necessarily argue for a divine ontology of three-ness (or thirty-three-ness). In the context of traditional Trinitarian thought, Dr. Richardson is surely correct in holding that all forms of religious experience point to God in his relations to the world and not to the internal relations in his being. Therefore, and this is still Richardson's argument, a trinity of distinctions where all distinctions refer to God's relations to the world are not, in fact, ontological distinctions, but simply references to the single divine mode of being related to the world.

Richardson's thesis is that genuine ontological distinctions must be restored to Trinitarian thought; a redemptive faith must, of necessity, apply the absolute categories to God as well as the relative ones. If God is "so involved in his creation that the victory over

---

[57] Cf the argument of K.E. Kirk, "The Vision of God" in A.E.J. Rawlinson, ed., *Essays on the Trinity & Incarnation*, (London, New York : Longmans, Green, 1928), pp. 157-237.

sin is not already his", then God is not really God";[58] that is, God
is not God unless he provides an absolutely stable and certain ground
for our faith. Nevertheless, that "God does become involved in
suffering for the world's redemption... is the very heart of the Christian
gospel".[59] Therefore, we must conceive of God as absolute and (at
the same time and without any tinge of subordination) as dynamically
involved in the world.

Several crucial issues in our understanding of God have now
come to a head. The movement of Trinitarian thought towards
involving the whole trinity with the world is a movement at variance
with the Hellenic insistence upon the absolute character of deity.
Richardson's mediating position that trinitarianism must be rethought
in order to assert, paradoxically, both the relativity and the absoluteness of deity has the value of affirming God's dynamic relation
to the world without threatening the religious confidence in God's
redeeming power. Nevertheless, there are some problems here.
Richardson's formulation serves to remind us of the logical difficulties in the concept of the absolute. These difficulties have rami-
fications well beyond Trinitarian thought, and must be examined before any decision can be made regarding the meaning of the
Trinitarian distinctions. Secondly, the meaning of redemption is
not entirely clear, so that it is not immediately evident that only the
category of the absolute can protect the redemptive functions of
God. We had better first examine what redemption can mean
and then speak of how God acts redemptively. Finally, there is
the problem of the meaning of Trinitarian thought. Are there valid
theological and philosophical grounds for moving towards a relational notion of deity? If there are, then what are we to make of
the Trinitarian distinctions of this ancient dogma?

The means by which I come at these several problems can most
accurately be described as a Whiteheadian critique of Thomas
Aquinas. Of course the choice of Aquinas and Whitehead is neither
arbitrary nor by chance. In the history of the idea of God, Aquinas'
thought exemplifies the systematic application of the logic of the
absolute to the Biblical picture of God. Thus his thought provides
a supremely adequate basis against which to examine the contention

---

[58] Cyril Richardson, "The Ontological Trinity : Father and Son", *Religion
in Life*, XXIX, Winter 1959-60, p. 12.
[59] Richardson, *The Doctrine of the Trinity*, p. 122.

of my argument : namely, that the serious problems that surround the traditional concept of God have their roots in absolutist modes of thinking. Two working principles inform the character of this critical examination. The first is that the philosophic reason for questioning a concept of God is the *absurdum* to which its logical implications reduce us. The second, somewhat looser principle, is that the theological reason for questioning a concept of God is its failure to be adequate to the Biblical picture of God.

Despite the fact that the discussion of Aquinas is handled apart from its historical context, there is of course a "pre-understanding" involved in the critique of his doctrines which is rooted in a difference of historical perspective. In the preface I suggested that it is now an historical possibility to think out a doctrine of God predicated upon the principle of relativity and that, indeed ,work has already started along these lines. This possibility of a reconception of God, specifically one grounded in a Whiteheadian perspective, informs the critique of the divine properties at every step and finally forms the basis for working out a social view of deity within a redemptive and trinitarian faith. Against the still widespread assumption that White-head's thought is not available to Christian faith, the argument of this book is that the Whiteheadian perspective does not reject the problems set by Aquinas but seeks to meet them more adequately. Thus the Whiteheadian view could be seen as a modification of rather than a rejection of the tradition.

CHAPTER II

GOD'S BEING AND THE LOGIC OF KNOWING

Aquinas' doctrine of God is systematic; that is, it is interlocking in nature and all-inclusive in aim. Given the modest scope and intention of this critique, it is neither possible nor necessary to examine every aspect of Aquinas' concept of God. What I propose to do in these several chapters devoted to Aquinas is to draw out those problems which lie within the doctrines of divine knowledge, will, power, perfection, and simplicity.

First, I wish to point out the dual methodology and epistemology which underlie Aquinas' doctrine of omniscience. The principles of knowing, derived from an empirical method and applicable to the human mode of knowing, are simply abandoned by Aquinas where the knower is God. The metaphysical ground for such an abandonment is the presupposition that God is an exception to ontological principles; the methodology found applicable to such an exception is, of necessity, deductive rationalism, and the epistemology found appropriate is an idealistic one. Let me establish these points and then draw out their logical, but problematic, implications.

Aquinas holds that "the reason why we actually feel or know a thing is because our intellect or sense is actually informed by the sensible or intelligible species... it follows (then) that sense or intellect is distinct from the sensible or intelligible object".[1] Thus, the very pre-requisite of knowledge is the presence of multiple things; knowledge itself occurs where there is a self-conscious subject consciously

---

[1] St. Thomas Aquinas, *Summa Theologica*, E.T. English Dominican Fathers (London : Burns, Oates & Washburne, Ltd. 1916-1938), Ia, 14.2. cf. St. Thomas Aquinas, *Summa Contra Gentiles*, E.T., Anton Pegis, (Doubleday, Garden City, New York, 1955-1957), I, 77.5 : "Knowledge takes place, according as the known is in some way in the knower".

distinguishing the individuals amongst the many of the world. Knowledge then involves activity insofar as it requires the ability to grasp distinctions; it involves passivity in that it is dependent upon or relative to the experiencing of sensible objects external to it. That the epistemology here is "realistic" and the methodology empirical is clear enough. The difficulty comes in with Aquinas' complete reversal of himself on these points in regard to the divine mode of knowledge.

God's "intellect", Aquinas holds, "and its objects are altogether the same... nor does the intelligible species differ from the substance of the divine intellect... but the intelligible species itself is the divine intellect itself".[2] Further, "What lies outside Himself, God does not see except in Himself"; similarly, "things other than Himself are known by God not in themselves but in Himself".[3] Hence, in God, the known is the knower, the object is the subject, the external is the internal. This collapse of distinctions rids God's knowing of all elements of passivity, dependence, and relativity so that it can be conceived of as an absolute act. Still, in order to achieve this conception Aquinas had to move from a realistic epistemology to an idealistic one. That is, in the ordinary (realistic) case, the subject gains knowledge from experiencing things external to it; in the divine (idealistic) case, knowledge of outside things is attained by self-contemplation. Aquinas justifies this shift by deductively reasoning from the unquestioned assumption of God's absoluteness of being. To protect the divine absoluteness it is necessary that God's knowledge, in toto, be idealistically based. Methodological inconsistency, however, has a price and in this case it lands Aquinas' thought into some serious logical and moral problems.[4]

Consider the following argument. "In science and in sense", Aquinas writes, "a real relation exists (with regard to the knower) because they are ordered either to the knowledge or to the sensible perception of things".[5] That is, in the ordinary case, knowledge

---

[2] Summa Ia, 14.2.

[3] Summa Ia, 14.5.

[4] I am indebted to Charles Hartshorne for the main lines of this argument. Cf. Charles Hartshorne and William Reese, eds. *Philosophers Speak of God*, (Chicago and London, The University of Chicago Press, 1953), pp. 131 ff., and Charles Hartshorne, *The Divine Relativity*, A Social Conception of God, (New Haven : Yale University Press, 1948), pp. 6 ff.

[5] Summa Ia, 13.7.

conforms to its object, or, put another way, knowing depends upon the existence of the particular object of cognition. Thus, according to Aquinas' realistic epistemology, the knower is related to things which are what they are without regard to the fact that they are known. The particular things that are known do not depend for their existence upon the fact that they are known, but quite the reverse. Existence is not relative to the knower, but the knower incurs a genuine relation to the known. What is non-relative, then, in this scheme of understanding, are the objects of knowledge, and it would seem to follow that the degree of relativity varies directly with the amount of knowledge possessed by any particular mind. Since to be aware of something is to be related to it, it follows that nothing is so variously related or dependent as mind or awareness. From this empirically based principle of knowledge, the inevitable conclusion is that an all-knowing omniscient mind is a supremely relative mind. To say then that God is the supreme knower would seem to be saying that God is the supremely relative being.

This conclusion, of course, runs head-on into the presupposition of the divine absoluteness. The logic of such a presupposition leads Aquinas to affirm that "in God there is no real relation to creatures".[6] But to hold that a supreme knower is not supremely relative, it is necessary to reverse the principles of knowledge where God is concerned, with the result that the word knowing has no literal common meaning when applied to God and man. Aquinas, of course, believes that it has an analogical meaning, but this itself is questionable, for as Hartshorne points out "it is an analogy which inverts the two terms (knower and known) giving the 'subject' the very role taken, in the ordinary case, by the object".[7] For example, in the ordinary case of knowing, real knowledge corresponds to, and therefore is relative to existent objects, but in the divine case, existent objects correspond to, and therefore are relative to knowing. "The knowledge of God", Aquinas writes, "is the cause of things... God causes things by his intellect".[8] In the divine case, then, it is misleading to say that the knower knows what is; rather, things are, because the knower knows them. Divine knowledge then creates beings, but derives nothing from the concrete beings created. In

[6] *Ibid.*, Ia, 13.7.

[7] Hartshorne & Reese, *op. cit.*, p. 120.

[8] Summa Ia, 14.8.

sum, concrete existence is absolutely relative to or dependent upon divine knowledge whereas divine knowledge is absolutely non-relative to or non-dependent upon concrete existence.

This kind of analysis raises the problem of the meaning of language when applied to God. To know, in the ordinary meaning of the term, involves the relativity of subject to object while in the divine case, it involves the relativity of object to subject. Thus, by inverting the terms of the relationship, the logical structure of the analogy is severely strained and the question is whether this strain does not wreck the correspondence. For if being and nature in any given case is said to depend upon knowing, then, knowing, in that particular case, is being used to signify the opposite of its ordinary meaning.

Perhaps a more serious question is whether the inversion of terms in the knower-known relationship vitiates the applicability of the term "subject" to God. The problem is whether a non-relative subject involves either a contradiction in terms, or, at the least, inferior subjectivity. Let us examine the point.

Aquinas holds that relations "are in God only in idea";[9] that is, they are not real relations but logical ones; they are external to the divine being, rather than internal to it. The provided example of such a relationship is that of the animal standing on the right side of a column. "On the right", Aquinas notes, "is not applied to a column unless it stands as regards an animal on the right side; which relation is not really in the column but in the animal... (and) as a column is on the right of an animal without change in itself, but by change in the animal, (relation can be) predicated of God, not by any change in Him, but by reason of the change of the creature".[10] The animal, then, may change its position in relation to the column, so that the column may be said to be now on the right, now on the left of the animal, but, in fact, nothing happens to the column by virtue of this relative change in the animal's position, whereas something does happen to the animal. Aquinas' conclusion is that the animal is relative to the column, whereas the column is non-relative to the animal. A corresponding relationship, Aquinas argues, holds between God and the creatures.

Now by the very nature of an analogy, it cannot be pushed too far without breaking down, but consider the implications of this

[9] Summa Ia, 13.7.
[10] Summa Ia, 13.7.

one. What is non-relative here is a fixed, inorganic, unaware, stone object; what is relative is a moving, organic, aware subject. Precisely because the animal takes relations into account, we consider it a subject; and conversely, precisely because of its non-relative character, the column is considered an object. It would seem to follow that the degree of subjectivity varies directly with the extent of relatedness, and conversely, the degree of objectivity varies directly with the extent of non-relatedness. Absurd inferences abound here : either we end up conceiving God as similar to a supreme object rather than a supreme subject or we maintain that subject in the divine case is sheerly opposite in meaning to what it means in its ordinary usage. This fact is hardly mitigated by arguing that the term subject is being used analogically when applied to God. For analogy involves the correspondence of meaning between two terms, and this cannot be reconciled with meanings which turn out to be structurally opposite.

It can be argued that the analogy of God to a fixed and unaware object is a deficient one to begin with, for God is supremely rich in awareness and life. But this would be to miss the point of the inevitable unacceptability of any analogy drawn between God and a non-relative thing. Subjectivity, or awareness, in our experience always involves real relations; they are variables of each other. Consider the following analogy and its corresponding argument formulated by Hartshorne.[11] Plato influenced the thought hand writings of Kant and Leibniz, but is himself independent of any real relationship to them. That is, Leibniz and Kant are relative to Plato, Plato is non-relative or absolute to them. But note that Plato's independence of relationship here rises out of his ignorance of his successors in their individuality (Plato certainly possessed the general knowledge that he would influence others), and that if Plato was familiar in a concrete way with his successors, they would have qualified his own thought and writing. In other words it is as ignorant that Plato is non-relative (or absolute) in relation to his successors, and it is as knowing that his successors are relative to him. Again, the conclusion is that supreme knowledge would seem to involve supreme relatedness. This conclusion can, of course, be mitigated by the argument that God, in his eternality, knows all events, past, present and future, in their individuality. The task, then, is to determine whether such knowledge is a logical possibility.

[11] Cf. Hartshorne, *The Divine Relativity*, pp. 16 ff.

Aquinas would argue that if a subject has present in his intellect universal concepts through which individuals are known as parts, then this mode of knowing effectively allows knowledge of other things without involving real relations with them. Now for Aquinas "other things are in God as in their common and universal cause, and are known by God as in their first and universal cause".[12] This is to know things generally and not in their individuality and, therefore, Aquinas presents two main arguments for God's pre-vision of all events in their distinctness and concreteness.[13] First, creaturely perfections wholly pre-exist in God, who is their ground. Since distinctions in things belong to their perfection, distinction or concreteness pre-exist in God. Second, the nature proper to each particular thing consists in some degree of participation in the divine perfection. As God knows himself, or the nature of being, perfectly, he must also know all particular modes of beings. The deductive and abstract character of this argument need hardly be pointed out, but its main deficiency is, perhaps, that it simply begs the question whether the character of an actual, concrete event is such that it is irreconcileable with any deductive argument for its pre-existence.

Aquinas quite rightly holds that God must know things in their particularity for "to know a thing in general and not in particular is to have an imperfect knowledge of it".[14] Also there is no reason to disagree with Aquinas on the score that "in God there exists the most perfect knowledge",[15] but there is a question whether perfect knowledge can mean anything more than the maximum possible knowledge. Now Aquinas draws no distinction between possible knowledge and knowledge which encompasses all durations; for he assumes that by predicating God as necessarily infinite and eternal, God must possess all truths, abstract and concrete ones, in a timeless manner. The analogy of proportion holds here : divine knowledge, being in accordance to an eternal mode of being, must, from eternity, fully anticipate all later states in earlier ones. Nevertheless, since Aquinas recognizes the world as contingent and not necessary, he must reconcile timeless, necessary divine knowledge with a contingent,

---

[12] Summa Ia, 14.6.
[13] Summa Ia, 14.6.
[14] Summa Ia, 14.6.
[15] Summa Ia, 14.1.

partially indeterminate world. Put very baldly, his problem is how God can know as determinate what is as yet only a somewhat indeterminate potentiality.

Aquinas recognized that a contingent thing considered as it is in its own cause or causes, that is, considered as future and not yet determined to one outcome, is not subject to any certain knowledge.[16] Therefore, he holds that "God knows all contingent things not only as they are in their causes, but also as each one of them is actually in itself".[17] That is, God knows a future contingent thing not as future, but as now in act as an already determined one. "God knows contingent things not successively but simultaneously" he writes (because) "God's knowledge is measured by eternity, as is also His being; and eternity being simultaneously whole comprises all time".[18] We are at the root of Aquinas' dualistic epistemology : what cannot be certain to time bound creatures (who know future contingent things as such) is certain to God, whose understanding is of the eternal order, and for whom all contingent events are present in the single divine vision of things.

Aquinas' intent here is not to argue that what is a contingent or possible event from our viewpoint is a necessary one from God's. Aquinas would want to affirm that God knows the contingent as contingent, the possible as possible, and the necessary as necessary. A definition of these terms might be helpful here. The necessary is that which is derived from the essential structure of a being; for instance, the properties of a sphere are absolutely necessary. What is possible is that which might have occurred, but did not, or which might occur, but will not; what is contingent is that which could have been different from what it is. According to this scheme, a contingent event did not have to be, but once it is, it is an actual fact and as such can be known infallibly as a true event. Since God's mode of knowing is informed by His eternal mode of being, God infallibly knows all contingent events as contingent in an eternal now.[19]

The argument is ingenious, but somewhat facile, for it raises the question of the logical possibility of necessary knowledge containing contingent occurrences. If God knows contingent events as contingent,

---

[16] Summa Ia, 14.13.
[17] Summa Ia, 14.13.
[18] Summa 14.13.
[19] Cf. C. G. 1, 67.2 ff.

then what He knows as contingent, if contingent is to retain its meaning, He knows as that which might not occur. Should it not occur, God cannot have known it as occurring without falling into error. Now Aquinas deals with the problem of possible but non-occurring events under the rubric of "whether God has knowledge of things that are not".[20] He argues here that God has two modes of knowing : knowing by vision which extends over all time and to all existing things, and knowing by intelligence which extends to all unrealized potentialities and possibilities. In other words, there is a distinction in the divine intellect between actual and conceptual knowledge. Applying this distinction to the problem of necessary knowledge containing contingent events, it would appear that God distinguishes in a single eternal vision genuine possibilities from actual occurrences. But this solution tends to make a muddle of language and logic. For a possibility to be a genuine possibility there must be a likelihood of its actual occurrence. But Aquinas' analysis forbids this, for he holds that those things which God knows as possibles have no possibility for realization. He defines the possibles as "those things which are not, nor will be, nor were".[21] The upshot of this is that in regard to actualization a possible must be an impossible. Thus, once again we have an example of a term which, in the context of divine knowledge, is given a meaning opposite to that of its ordinary usage. Aside from the linguistic muddle, this analysis raises the question whether possibles, in the common understanding of the term, exist at all. That is, can the process of the world be anything other it is?

Aquinas understands the nature of divine knowledge as such that no other world than this one is possible other than in conception. Consider the implication of this interpretation.[22] God would possess the infallible knowledge that world W is actual, world W' only possible. But this knowledge is logically incompatible with the inactuality of world W and with the actuality of world W'. If divine knowledge is necessary then the inactuality of world W and the actuality of world W' is necessarily impossible. In a word, if possible is not simply to lose its meaning there are no possible worlds and this world is as necessary as God. Thus, to assert the necessity of

---

[20] Summa Ia, 14.9.

[21] Summa Ia, 14.9.

[22] Again, my debt for the following argument is to Hartshorne. Cf. Hartshorne, *The Divine Relativity*, pp. 12 ff.

divine knowledge is to imply the necessity of the world, and this is to do away with all contingency whatsoever. Everything is necessary or God's eternal knowledge may be open to error. What then has happened to Aquinas' distinction between necessary and contingent?

In the context of the discussion on divine knowledge Aquinas affirms that a contingent event, known simply in its causes, is not subject to any certain knowledge. In this manner, he tentatively preserves the meaning of "contingent" though he later significantly develops and modifies the argument. "It is not because the proximate causes are contingent" he writes, "that the effects willed by God happen contingently, but because God has prepared contingent causes for them, it being his will that they should happen contingently".[23] Further, he notes that "whatsoever divine providence ordains to happen infallibly and of necessity happens infallibly and of necessity; and that happens from contingency which the plan of divine providence conceives to happen from contingency".[24] Now saying that knowledge of causes does not yield certain knowledge of events has quite different implications from saying that "effects willed by God happen contingently... because God has prepared contingent causes for them". The first statement is compatible with the view that the total conditions prior to the actualization of a contingent event do not dictate the outcome of the event; the second implies the presence of an ultimate condition which determines events. In other words, an event is contingent in that it depends upon God for its existence, but no event is contingent in the sense that it might not have happened.[25] Aquinas' understanding of the divine will and divine knowledge as "perfectly efficacious"[26] is finally compatible only with the deterministic view of things. Jacques Maritain, in a short article,[27] echoes this aspect of Aquinas when he notes, with approval, the view that contingent events are "infal-

[23] Summa Ia, 19.8.

[24] Summa Ia, 22.4., cf. C. G. I, 85.6.

[25] Cf. St. Thomas Aquinas, *Commentary on the Metaphysics of Aristotle*, E.T.J. Rowan (Chicago : Henry Regnery Co., 1961), VI, 3.1220.

[26] Cf. Summa Ia, 19.3 : "not only that things are done, which God wills to be done, but also that they are done in the way that He wills". Cf. also *Commentary on the Metaphysics of Aristotle*, VI, 3.1218 : "These two statements are incompatible, namely that something is foreknown by God and that it does not come to pass".

[27] Jacques Maritain, "Reflections on Necessity and Contingency", in Robert E. Brennan, O. P., ed., *Essays in Thomism* (New York : Sheed & Ward, 1942).

libly predetermined in the constellation and the history of all the factors that were posited in the beginning".[28] Thus, he can simply assert that, to the divine intellect, a contingent event "would appear as an infallibly or necessarily determined event".[29]

Nevertheless, this understanding of divine knowledge shows some sign of straining against itself when Aquinas seeks to affirm the infinity of the divine knowledge. The reason for this is that in the context of the idea of infinity, Aquinas discovers that he must argue not only for the knowledge of the existence of actuals in the divine intellect, but for the knowledge of genuine possibles as well – even the knowledge of the possible existence of a better world than this.[30] The seed of revolution is here, but because the idea of pure actuality triumphs, the possibles are not possible at all, but become understood as necessarily inactualizeable.[31]

In sum, though Aquinas' intention is to retain the language and the reality of the contingency of events (i.e. particular events do not have to occur), the logic of the character of divine knowledge inevitably leads to the contradiction that contingent events are necessary occurrences. Though Aquinas means to understand God as a supremely transcendent subject, his inversion of the knower-known relationship, in the divine case, implies that either God bears closer analogical resemblance to a supreme object or that he is inferior in subjectivity or awareness. Even if we accept the extreme view of some recent Thomistic studies that for Aquinas "there are no analogous concepts but only inadequate notions which we can use to 'intend to mean' what we want to say about God",[32] it still will not do to blur linquistic distinctions so hopelessly that contingency fails to contrast with necessity, that possibles are understood as unrealizeables, and that subject is confused with object. To give to theological language meanings which are sheerly opposite from their common usage is hardly a proper way to proceed in saying what we "intend to mean", nor does the acknowledgement that

[28] *Ibid.*, p. 29.

[29] *Ibid.*, p. 27.

[30] Summa Ia, 25.6, Re. obj. 3.

[31] Cf. Frederick Sontag, *The Divine Perfection*, (New York, Harper, 1961), pp. 47 ff., for a detailed discussion on this point.

[32] David Burrell, "Kant & Philosophical Knowledge", *The New Scholasticism*, XXXVIII, 2, April, 1964, p. 211.

our concepts about God are necessarily inadequate provide a blanket excuse for such a complete breakdown in linguistic usage and logic. If the argument is that the very nature of divine perfection produces such apparent illogicalities in language and thought – because God "measures events by eternity", whereas "our event language is irreducibly tensed" [33] – then surely the task of religious thought is to re-examine our "inadequate notions" of divine being. If they are "inadequate", there is nothing sacrosanct about them, and the role of scholarship is, after all, to achieve lesser degrees of inadequacy. To rest content with the illogical consequences of theological formulations is either to imply the ultimate untrustworthiness of our logic or the illogical structure of the very ground of our being. On the other hand, to reject both these implications is not necessarily to deny the ultimate mystery of being. There can be a middle position where reason is informed by faith, but where, nevertheless, the logical demands of reason constitute a norm for the understanding in its ongoing search for truth. Thought cannot demonstrate the ground for such a norm, but it is the very pre-supposition to thought.

My own view then is that many of the theological paradoxes or logical contradictions which are part of the furniture of the orthodox conception of omniscience can be sloughed off by qualifying the sheerly absolute character of the divine knowledge. Thus we can begin by not draining off all meaning from Aquinas' assertion that God knows the contingent as contingent and the possible as possible. An event which is possible might or might not occur, and therefore cannot be known, even by a supreme knower, except as in a state of indeterminacy. An event which is contingent, might not have occurred, and had it not occurred, it could not have been known by a supreme intelligence as having occurred. If future event X is not a necessary event, then not X must be a real possibility. For God to know possible events as possible must mean, then, that he knows X and not X in conception. That is, a supreme knower would have infallible knowledge of all possible outcomes of an event, and in this sense, he is omniscient – in this sense, nothing can take him by surprise. But since some possible events are incompatible with others (X is incompatible with not X) until one or another occurs, God can

[33] David Burell, "Aristotle and Future Contingencies", *Philosophical Studies*, XIII, 1964, p. 50.

only know all possibles in conception and none in actuality. Thus, this view agrees with Aquinas that we must ascribe an infinity of possibles to the divine intellect, and that we must assert that there are other things in God's knowledge than those things which have proved, and will prove, themselves actualized. The difference comes in taking the logic of the argument seriously and not allowing a prior understanding of deity as pure actuality and in zero dependence upon the world to dictate its conclusion. To grant the contingency of the world, then, is to imply that knowledge which is absolute in adequacy to all possible future events must be knowledge which is deficient in reality; i.e. it is not knowledge of actual events. Thus, to envision all possible events is precisely not to know future events in their actualized particularity. In other words, a perfect knower would not know the future in its concrete details, for in a contingent world, the concrete details are only given in the now of the present. In saying that knowledge of concrete things involves temporality, I am arguing for two aspects in the divine being : an abstract and eternal one by which God knows all necessary truths and envisions all general possibilities, and a concrete one which is consequent or relative to the particular events thrown up by the actual temporal world. In other words, this view does maintain an absolute or non-relative aspect in God's knowledge, not only in the weak sense that God knows "the eternal truths of reason", but also in regard to the full adequacy of the divine mind to any possible totality of conditions. No event can relativize the adequacy of God's knowledge, though in knowing any actual event, God is related to and relativized by that event. The distinction is that between the (abstract) type of relationship God has to any event and His (concrete) knowledge of any actual event.

The argument that relative knowledge implies an imperfection in the knower overlooks the fact that human knowledge is imperfect, not because of its relative or dependent character but because of its limited scope or insufficient relativity, and its limited vision or insufficient imagination. Thus, at any point in the ongoing world process, God knows concretely and certainly every actuality which exists to be known, and He knows abstractly and generally the infinite range of all real possibilities. God remains, then, "the measure of all truth"; but this statement, as Hartshorne points out, must be restricted to mean that God alone "can establish a perfect corre-spondence between his knowing and what He knows, or between what He knows to be, and what they are".[34] What has been abandoned are those aspects of the doctrine of omniscience which imply that God can know what cannot be known : namely, an actual event prior to its achieving concrete actuality.

What is at stake here is more than the question of the meaning of perfect knowledge or the logic of theological thinking. My concern with the kind of logic which turns possibles into impossibles, and contingencies into necessities is not simply its muddled character but also its ethical implications. For what is endangered in draining out the ordinary meaning from words such as knowing, contingent, and possible, when these terms are applied to God, is man's freedom of choice and moral responsibility. To insist that God knows from eternity all possible events which will not be actualized is ultimately to deny that any given event had an alternative outcome. To hold that the exact plan of actualization is known in an eternally present now is to imply an ontologically useless creation lacking in freedom and responsibility. Subtle interpretations can be made to mitigate the dark side of orthodoxy and to shore up Thomistic logic. The argument of the following chapters is that such interpretations miss the point because the logical and moral problems in Aquinas' concept of God, stem not from any particular obscurities in Aquinas' thought, but from the category of the absolute which informs his doctrine of God.

[34] Hartshorne, *The Divine Relativity*, p. 12.

CHAPTER III

GOD'S WILL AND ONTOLOGICAL ARBITRARINESS

The informing concept of divine absoluteness provides its own peculiar problems to the doctrine of God's will. The task here is to set forth the problems and Thomas' resolution of them, and then to examine the doctrine critically by uncovering its implications.

The initial problem lies in finding a mid-way point between the denial that an end or aim informs the divine will and the straightforward assertion that the absolutely perfect and sheerly inner determined divine being is, in fact, determined by an end. To deny that God has an enduring end not only deprives deity of its moral moorings, but subjects the divine will to either blind necessity or arbitrariness. On the other hand, the assertion that God has an end compromises either the divine completeness of being (God as pure act) or the divine independence of being (God as *a se*).

Consider the stickness of the problem from Aquinas' point of view : the straightforward moral assertion that God's end is the good of the other or that God's end is the harmony of the universal community, suggests that the world is as necessary to God as God to the world. Indeed, it can be argued that any conception of end from a moral or social perspective would involve deity in ontological dependence, for such a perspective is a relational one : *viz*, moral and social perspectives involve the good, and therefore the existence, of a community of beings. Nor can Aquinas solve the problems by conceiving of God's end as a "yet to be realized" divine state of being, for this admits incompleteness and (provisional) imperfections in deity.

The problem for Aquinas then is two-fold : the moral integrity of deity must be affirmed without the implication of divine relativity; the concept of divine end must be maintained without admitting incompleteness of being into deity.

Thomas meets the problem head on by holding that God's end is not apart from the perfection of his goodness, which is his eternally realized being. The Summa formally states it this way :

they object of the divine will is His goodness, which is His essence. Since the will of God is His essence, it is not moved by another than itself, but by itself alone.[1]

We have lived so long with this answer that we are liable not only to miss its brilliance, but its problematic character as well. God's moral integrity is affirmed by holding that God wills the good of things other than himself; relativity of deity is avoided by arguing that what moves God, namely, the divine end, is not the will to the good of the other, but God's own goodness. The paradigm of the divine will, here, is the same as that of God's knowledge of things other than himself : as God "understands things apart from Himself by understanding His own essence, so He wills things apart from Himself by willing His own goodness".[2] In this way, the divine completeness is also assured. God's willing things apart from Himself is not distinct from, but derivative to His willing His own goodness. Similarly, the divine end, in respect to the willing of other things, is not distinct from God's own end which is His eternal perfection of being. In other words, God not only wills nothing necessarily other than Himself, but, also, whatever He wills, He wills with respect to His own end.

Gilson argues, in support of the Thomist concept of God, that precisely because God is the actuality of pure being or being itself, it cannot be conceived that God could have any other end than Himself.[3] True enough, if God is pure (absolute) being, but Gilson's argument simply exemplifies the pitfall of the deductive and rationalistic character of the Thomist and neo-Thomist mode of theologizing. The cogency of the notion "pure actuality of being" is simply assumed as established by the proofs and its cogency is never seriously examined by a critical analysis of its implications. In any event, that is the task here : to pursue the logic of the Thomist position on the divine will and to examine the logical moral and religious tenability of its implications.

---

[1] Summa Ia, 19.1.

[2] Ibid., 19.2

[3] Etienne Gilson, The Spirit of Medieval Philosophy, E. T., A. C. Downes, (New York : Charles Scribner's, 1940), pp. 92-93.

By holding that God wills everything with respect to Himself and that God's end is not apart from his being, Aquinas provisionally avoids implying an ontological reciprocity between God and world. But this identification of God's will and end with God Himself threatens to drain these two terms of their very meaning. In one aspect of their meaning both will and end presuppose a partially unrealized state of being or a potency or openness to being. Thus we speak of will as that aspect of the self which drives the self to attain what it does not possess; namely, an end outside itself. Thomas rejects this understanding of the relation between will and end as being inappropriate to deity. He argues that in the divine case will is more properly understood in its sense as "the love and delight in what it does possess".[4] Thomas may have in mind here such general psychological states as the will to live, wherever life is found, the will to power where power is possessed, the will to happiness, where happiness is already achieved.

The difficulty with this argument is that we tend to judge a will as morally defective where the end of that will is sheerly the maintenance of the subject's psychological state of being. What morally justifies a being's life, power, happiness, etc., is not the being's "love and delight in what it does possess" but the going out towards the good of the other in life, power, happiness, etc., In other words, to speak of will, independent of a social context, is to speak either of an abstract will, or a morally deficient one. The point is, the will achieves its moral dimension only within a concrete communal situation involving mutually responsible selves.

If the above argument is correct, then to say that God's will does not essentially involve the going out toward the good of the other is to threaten to empty the concept of God of its moral integrity. The question is not whether the divine will can be so conceived – obviously it has been so conceived at the very center of the Christian tradition – but whether such a conception is morally and religiously tolerable to a faith informed by the life and words of Jesus Christ. For example, can a will, independent of relations, be conceived as perfect within a doctrine of God which places the Johannine statement that God is love at its center? [5] Love, however we define it, involves

---

[4] Summa Ia., 19.1.

[5] Perhaps the difficulty in Thomas' thought here is partly grounded in methodology; i.e., the Biblical affirmation of divine love gets discussed only after the philosophical concept of God has been worked out.

the concern of one being for another so that the affirmation that God is love grounds God's moral integrity precisely in the affirmation that His will essentially and primarily is the will toward the good of the other. The argument that the social context of will is appropriate only to the creature and not the creator can only serve to raise the question whether love informs the divine will. The issue here, however, is not whether Aquinas' concept of will is adequately informed by Biblical faith, but whether any concept of will can elude the amoral and the arbitrary unless it is grounded in a social context where the self responsibly goes out towards the other in sympathy and concern.

Significantly enough, there is a moment in Thomas' thought where he sees and accepts the thrust of this kind of argument, though he does not draw out its ontological implications. I am referring to that point where Thomas recognizes that the assertion of the sufficiency of God's perfect goodness to his will fails to allow adequate ground for God's willing things apart from himself.[6] Aquinas' argument is sufficiently pertinent to the discussion here to merit quoting in full. He writes :

Natural things have a natural inclination not only towards their own proper good, to acquire it if not possessed, and, if possessed, to rest therein; but also to spread abroad their own good amongst others, so far as possible. Hence every agent in so far as it is perfect and in act, produces its like. It pertains therefore to the nature of the will, to communicate as far as possible to others the good possessed; and especially does this pertain to the divine will, from which all perfection is derived in some kind of likeness... (i.e.) it pertains to the divine will to communicate by likeness its own good to others as much as is possible.[7]

Here is the clear recognition that in both the creaturely and divine instance the will is to be understood as naturally inclined to and concerned with the good of others; i.e., the will, in the fullness or actuality of its being, is to be understood as the moral-social will. Thus, to hold that "it pertains to the nature of the will to communicate as far as possible to others the good possessed", is to imply that to communicate the good is a perfection of being. And since Thomas specifically argues that the will to communicate the good "especially" pertains to the divine will, we have the explicit denial

---

[6] Summa Ia, 19.2.
[7] *Ibid.*, Ia, 19.2.

that this is but another case where God is an exception to ontological principles.

At this point in Thomas' thought, then, the logic of his argument suggests that the concept of divine will requires the existence of others as a class; in other words, it requires a social nexus. Aquinas, for reasons of logic and dogma, never comes to this social view of deity. First, he never explicitly distinguished between the necessity of a class of things and the necessity of the actuality of particular members within a class. These two are of a logically different order : a class referring to an abstract entity, a particular member referring to a concrete actuality. The point is that necessity of class does not logically require the existence of any actual member within that class. Thomas' failure to realize this distinction precluded his recognition that the idea that God alone is the only necessary actual entity is not logically incompatible with the necessity of a class of things. Secondly, for dogmatic reasons, Thomas is convinced that the logic of the arguments for God's existence does not allow for any compromise with respect to God's absolute independence of being. This dogmatic conviction informs all his thought, and overcomes any arguments, even his own, which might imply the contrary. Thus, in turning to consider whether God wills anything necessarily other than himself, what informs his thought is not his immediately previous analysis on the nature of will, but his conception of the meaning of divine perfection. What he says is this : "since the goodness of God is perfect and can exist without other things inasmuch as no perfection can accrue to Him from them, it follows that His willing things apart from Himself is not absolutely necessary".[8] That "the goodness of God is perfect", is not here being questioned. The real question is whether perfect goodness, apart from a social context, can refer to anything more than an abstract structure of being deficient in moral actuality.[9] In other words, what price in cogency does the concept of God pay by Aquinas' refusal to recognize and resolve the tension existing between his social analysis of the will and his understanding of perfection as independence and completion of being?

It is true that Thomas turns to the problem of the necessity of the world when he draws a distinction between "a thing said to be

[8] *Ibid.*, Ia, 19.3.

[9] The relation between the idea of God's goodness and the divine creativity is set forth in St. Thomas Aquinas, *On The Power of God*, E. T. English Dominican Fathers (Westminster, Md., Newman Press, 1952), S. 4 : "God wills creatures

necessary, absolutely, and (said to be necessary) by supposition".[10] God alone is willed necessarily in the absolute sense : the world is willed necessarily by supposition. Thus, Thomas holds that there is a sense in which it must be said that the actual existence of a world is required by the concept of divine will. What cripples this insight, and renders it irrelevant to the issue of God's moral integrity, is that it is informed not by the moral integrity and social nature of will, but by the notions of the absoluteness and perfect efficacity of the divine will. Thus, what Aquinas means by asserting that things apart from God are willed necessary by supposition is that whatever God wills with respect to other things must be because God has willed them.[11]

There are several problems here. The first is that this formulation simply avoids the issue of the ground by which God wills to will things apart from himself. The second is more crucial, for to conceive of "necessity of supposition" rather than "necessity of class" as the type of necessity appropriate to the world is to undercut the moral ground for God's will toward the world. What the "necessity of supposition" doctrine means is that apart from his own existence whatever God wills to be is grounded not in his essence, which is his goodness, but in his good pleasure. Or to state it somewhat differently : God's will, with respect to the being of the world, is rooted ultimately not in the integrity of the divine will but in the mystery of the will. In other words, Aquinas chooses at this point, for dogmatic reasons – namely, the presupposition of the absolute character of divine being – to allow the principle of sufficient reason to lapse. The issue, however, is surely not whether logic can dispel all metaphysical mystery, but whether, in this concrete instance, mystery is introduced illegitimately and with disastrous moral consequences for our understanding of God's relation to the world.

What I want to argue is that Aquinas' failure to argue for the essential reciprocity of God and world introduces an element of

---

to exist for His goodness' sake, namely that they may imitate and reflect it". Thomas' assumption here is that goodness can be actualized apart from communication with another being.

[10] Summa Ia, 19.3.

[11] Cf. Aquinas, *The Commentary on the Metaphysics of Aristotle*, VI, 3, 1216 : "It follows, then, that everything which occurs here insofar as it is related to the first divine cause is found to be ordained by it and not to be accidental, although it may be found to be accidental in relation to other causes".

moral arbitrariness into the concept of deity. For the God of Aquinas, whose will is perfectly efficacious, is ontologically free not only to will or not to will a world, but is also under no absolute obligation of integrity in regard to the quality of the goodness of the particular world he does choose to will. What this means, and Thomas is not dismayed by the prospect, is that the ethical quality of the world is irrelevant to the divine perfection and goodness. Neither the goodness nor perfections of the world add a whit to God's perfection or goodness, nor does the goodness and perfection of God require, in any strict sense, the goodness of the world. The situation, here, is that the logic of Aquinas' concept of God would not allow him to hold that God requires and therefore wills a maximally good world. Had he done so, he would have set an external condition for an unconditioned God. That is, God's creative will would have as its end not simply the perfection of his already realized essence, but the perfection of a world. The concept of God here comes to a crossroad. It can either be held that God's will to create is grounded in the value of the world's being – which would ultimately lead to a radical revision in the doctrine of God – or God's creative will can be grounded in ontological mystery -- which would protect the idea of absolute aseity but would introduce the element of ontological arbitrariness into the idea of God.

Aquinas, of course, countenanced no move requiring a revision of God's absolute character. Instead, and this reflects the integrity of his thought, he drives the idea of God to the verge of admitting moral arbitrariness into deity. I am referring to Thomas' admission that God could have willed to create, and could have created, a better universe than that which actually exists.[12] That this admission is but the logical implication of grounding God's will in mystery is obvious; the spelling out of the moral significance of this admission apparently had to wait for Robert Patterson's critical study of Thomas' doctrine of God. Patterson, drawing attention to Aquinas' position here, writes the following :

Evil has been declared by St. Thomas to be a mere negation, a defect of being, and God had therefore been freed from all responsibility for it. But it is now apparent that many, if not all, of the evils which infect the actual universe would have been absent from a better universe which the deity might have created in its stead had he chosen. Hence the presence of these evils in the actual world is the result of his arbitrary will.

[12] Cf. Summa Ia, 25.6; and De Pot. 3.16.

It is clear that St. Thomas does not conceive God to be under any obligation in the matter... neither (God's) justice nor his goodness can be impugned because he has not created something better. In other words, Aquinas' God is quite as much an ontological tyrant as the Allah of the Koran.[13]

Ontological tyranny is too strong a charge to lay against Aquinas' rationalist concept of God, but surely something has gone awry in a Christian analysis of deity where the outcome is a God who could forgo creating a better universe in order to create a worse one.

The root of the problem lies, in part, in Aquinas' inadequate analysis of the relation of divine power to creaturely power. The discussion of that point will have to wait for the following chapter, but, as I have been urging in this chapter, the problem is rooted also in Aquinas' refusal to locate any cause for the divine will other than God's good pleasure. "In no wise has the will of God a cause",[14] Thomas writes, and, though his intent is to protect the autonomy of God, the arbitrary dimensions of this doctrine break through not only in respect to the idea of possible alternative worlds, but in respect to such doctrines as predestination and providence. Thus, Thomas can write : "why (God) chooses some for glory and reprobates others has no reason except the divine will".[15] The moral sterility of an absolutist ontology bares itself here.

Certainly, Thomas sought to protect the divine will from subjection to moral arbitrariness by holding the divine perfection and goodness as its end and object. But by collapsing the divine will for the world into God's willing of himself [16] Aquinas thought strains against itself. Thus, in seeking to uncover the relation between God's will and the world's being he is torn between an analysis of the nature of the moral will and the analysis of the "a se" idea of God. The outcome of this tension is a victory for the Hellenic concept of absolute being; the notion that it is a perfection to communicate the good was refused ontological recognition. Thus, we are left to draw the conclusion that what it means to hold that God could have willed into actuality a better creation than he in

---

[13] Robert Patterson, *The Concept of God in the Philosophy of St. Thomas Aquinas*, (London : Allen, 1933), p. 439.

[14] Summa Ia, 19.5.

[15] Summa Ia, 23.5.

[16] Cf. C. G. I 76.8.

fact did, is that God chose not to will "the good possessed as far as possible".

The irony here, is that this very separation of God's will from God's goodness, which lays Aquinas' concept of God open to Patterson's charge of "ontological tyranny", is inadmissible on Thomist grounds. Aquinas explicitly holds that God's " will is His goodness which is His essence".[17] The appeal, then, to mystery (which is the only meaning to ascribe to such a term as God's "good pleasure") in respect to God's will is internally contradictory. Further, where the language of mystery leads, in fact, to the suggestion of moral arbitrariness, surely the task is not to cloak the issue by asserting the necessary limitedness and distortions of our finite knowledge, but to re-examine our first principles.

Now, the moral and logical problems that beset Aquinas' doctrine of divine will can be avoided by conceiving an ontological basis for God's relation to the world. The dogmatic reasons for rejecting this solution are legion, and I will turn to that issue in the final chapter. For the present, I wish to develop the positive logical grounds for the argument that the structure of the divine will requires the existence of an actual world for its own actualization.

The key to this argument lies in developing Thomas' own insight into the moral and communal nature of the will.[18] Thomas' thought here provides us with the clue that the communication of "the good possessed" is a perfection or property of the will. If the communication of the good is a perfection, then the failure to communicate it is a deficiency. The moral will, then, is moral only on the condition that it is a will going out towards other beings; it follows from this that the act of willing of a perfect being must be structured within a relational nexus, so that the very fact of willing presupposes a community of beings. If this reasoning is correct, then any statement with respect to the divine will which seems to exclude such a nexus will turn out to be, upon examination, an abstraction from the concrete, actual situation.

Consider, then, the statement that God wills Himself necessarily but wills nothing other than Himself necessarily. Utilizing Hartshorne's definition of necessary as "without alternative possibility",[19]

[17] Summa Ia, 19.1.

[18] Cf. Summa Ia, 19.2.

[19] Charles Hartshorne, *The Logic of Perfection*, (La Salle, Illinois : Open Court Publishing Company, 1962), p. 149.

the statement means that God's being alone is without possibility of non-existence, and all other beings have alternative possibilities. The issue is not whether this statement is true – I have no argument with its truth – but whether it can bear Thomas' interpretation that the world requires divinity, but divinity does not require the world. In other words, can the statement achieve cogency outside a relational nexus?

First, I want to argue that the second part of the statement – God wills nothing other than Himself necessarily – does not logically exclude the statement that some world is necessary. What it does exclude is the statement that God necessarily wills a particular world, or that certain specific beings other than God necessarily achieve actuality. In other words, God could exist without us, or any other group of specified beings, but that does not mean that God could exist were there no other beings. It is one thing to say that certain beings exist accidentally; it is another to say that accidental being is necessary. The sum of this argument is that God and world can be understood as mutual ontological implicates without logically requiring a particular world structure or a particular actuality. Further, to hold that a world is necessary, though the structure and particular actualities of the world are not, has the decided advantage of protecting not only the freedom of God but the freedom of the world as well. Consistently adhered to, this understanding contrasts sharply with, and urges the rejection of, Aquinas' concept "necessity of supposition". This concept, while sufficiently, even overzealously, protecting divine freedom fails to protect the world's freedom in holding that what God wills, seeing that he wills it, must necessarily be. By replacing "necessity of supposition" by "necessity of class" – some world, though no particular world – the freedom of the world is protected without detrimentally qualifying God's freedom.

Still, it remains to establish that the logic of the statement, God wills Himself necessarily, requires, for its cogency, a world and God as ontological implicates : i.e., it must be demonstrated that this statement is an abstraction from a relational nexus.

We can begin with the question "what is the content of God's willing Himself necessarily"; i.e., what is it that God wills without possibility of its non-existence? To answer, "God", is not to answer at all, for it tells us no more than we already know, and is dangerously close to being an answer empty of content. An essay of Hartshorne's suggests a meaningful answer; namely, that which is without possibility of nonexistence can only be "possibility itself". As Hartshorne persuasively argues, "there can be no such entity as the possibility that there might not be possibility".[20] It follows that what is willed necessarily is that entity constitutive of possibility itself. If the above reasoning is correct, then the way is open to revise the traditional meaning of the statement "God exists necessarily "so that it no longer excludes accidents from the divine life. What we can now say is that the necessary existence of God refers to the necessary inclusion of God in any possible state of affairs as the ground of possibility for that state of affairs.[21]

The crux of this argument is that a mode of being which is constitutive of possibility refers not only to a mode of being which is both eternal and necessary but also to one which is abstract. Possibility must have some structure, but that structure is strictly formal. In sum, the eternal and necessary aspect of God is one in which He is conceived as constitutive of possibility itself, but this aspect is a formal concept deficient in actuality. Thus, in order to arrive at the concrete, actual life of God, it is necessary to assume some concrete, living world to be known, experienced etc., of which God is both ground and consequent. In sum, God's actuality, and (some) world's actuality are given together; there is no getting behind one or the other.

Aquinas' error is twofold. First, he mistook the abstract will for the concrete. He interpreted the meaning of God's necessary willing of Himself to refer to a concrete willing, as if some concrete actuality was involved, as if it were an act rather than the logically necessary ground for any concrete act. Second, though he corrected Augustine in placing the perfection of act at the center of his concept of God rather than the perfection of immovability,[22] he never clearly saw that to be concretely in act means to be in relation. This error is

[20] *Ibid.*, p. 149.

[21] Cf. Alfred North Whitehead, *Science and the Modern World*, (New York : The Macmillan Company, 1925), ch. 11, for the extension of this line of reasoning. Whitehead's argument for God takes off from the fact that this world is characterized by a determinate order of being and by concrete, finite things, and not by an indiscriminate modal pluralism. God is that principle necessary to account for this fact of concreteness and limitation. In other words, God functions to limit boundless and indeterminate possibility in order to allow for concrete and definite actuality.

[22] Etienne Gilson, *The Christian Philosophy of St. Thomas Aquinas*, E.T., L. K. Shool, (New York : Sheed and Ward, 1939), p. 102.

crucial not only in laying the ground for the moral, logical and religious problems that beset the doctrine of will, but in creating intolerable tensions in all aspects of the doctrine of God. This charge will bear further substantiation in a later chapter; for the present, it is enough to suggest that though Aquinas rightly corrected Augustine in making act the ultimate category, he tried to understand act within the Augustinian ontology of eternity, an ontology of rest rather than of change. We are here at the heart of the problem.

CHAPTER IV

POWER AND CREATIVITY — PART I

God's power is perfect power. To say anything less is to be false to the idea of God; but what we have said other than the high abstraction "whatever God does, he does perfectly", is not entirely clear. Everything depends on how we define perfection. The way we realize an adequate definition is, however, complicated. On the one hand, the tradition has tended to assume that we cannot talk responsibly about divine power unless we have presupposed a definition of perfection; on the other hand we do not know whether a theological definition is cogent or not until we see whether it drives our thought into logical contradictions. The truth is that the only "substantial reason for rejecting a philosophical theory is the 'absurdum' to which it reduces us".[1] My concern in this chapter is with the logical, moral and religious *absurdum* to which Aquinas' understanding of the perfection of power reduces us. Three preliminary remarks of a methodological sort will serve to indicate the broad lines of the problems before us.

Aquinas defines perfection as "completed act".[2] Therefore, if God's power is perfect, by definition, "God is unable to do those things whose possibility entails passive potency";[3] which is to say that passive power is wholly lacking in deity. More than this, passivity itself is understood as a defect, an imperfection of being.[4] Yet, ironically, as I shall argue, Aquinas' analysis of active and passive power undermines his very assumption that God is pure act and that perfection excludes passivity.

[1] Alfred North Whitehead, *The Concept of Nature*, (Cambridge : Cambridge University Press, 1920), p. 38.

[2] C. G. I, 28.10.

[3] C. G. II, 25.2.

[4] Summa Ia, 25.1.

Aquinas defines passive power as "the principle of being acted upon by something else", active power as "the principle of acting upon something else".[5] From these definitions, it would seem to follow that active power must be exercised upon something which possesses the (passive) power to be acted upon, or to be influenced or controlled. However, passive power, in its turn, cannot be absolutely inert for it would be merely nothing if it possessed no active tendency of its own. The two aspects or forms of power apparently are implicates of each other, each logically requiring the other for its own meaning.[6] The intellect can indeed separate them, that is, consider each by itself, apart from the contextual whole, but when it does so, the intellect is abstracting from existence and is dealing with an abstract form and not an actual existent. Thus, when Aquinas holds that God is "pure act", he is making the questionable assumption that an abstraction can serve as a symbol for the concrete actuality of the full divine existence. There is another reason for questioning the enterprise of grounding ontological value judgments on what is separable in logic but not in actuality. If activity, in fact, presupposes passivity, why should the character of perfection be located exclusively in one form of power? It would seem that the quality of the use and reception of power rather than one of the abstract forms of power would characterize the norm of perfect power.

A problem of a similar nature arises if we begin with Aquinas' understanding of divine omnipotence as the extension of God's power to whatever is logically possible.[7] The notion of omnipotence, then, implies that there is no possible power lacking in deity. In fact, of course, Aquinas excludes passive power from God even though he understands passive power as one of the possible categories of power. The ground for this exclusion is not that passive power is in fact opposed to power, but that it is "opposed to act";[8] i.e., it is opposed to a prior definition of perfect power. The anomaly consequent upon this exclusion is that the perfect divine being lacks a form or type of power which is not only common to all beings but, as I shall later argue, is found in increasing intensity as one ascends

---

[5] Summa Ia, 25.1.

[6] Thomas' position, of course, is that power is twofold, and not that the two forms of power are mutual implicates.

[7] Summa Ia, 25.3-4; De Pot. 1.7. Note that Aquinas excludes the logically impossible from God's power.

[8] Summa Ia, 25.1.

the scale of being. Further, since "God is unable to do those things whose possibility entails passive potency",[9] it follows that he lacks the values which are a function of those acts involving passivity. Thus, whatever values are uniquely inherent in those acts which entail risk (of failure), real alternative decisions, openness to novelty, mutual relations, etc., must be found wanting in God, for all of these involve the passivity of power. The reason for this a priori exclusion of a whole host of values is Aquinas' assumption that imperfection is the failure to actualize some potentialities or, more accurately, to have potentialities. But if this definition of perfection becomes suspect because it excludes from God certain values which, as I shall argue, other criteria require then Aquinas' doctrine of divine omnipotence itself becomes suspect.

The third preliminary point concerns whether even within the framework of Aquinas' thought, the implication of divine passivity or potentiality does not arise. Consider the following paragraph :

in voluntary actions, power and knowledge are brought into action by the will; wherefore in God power and knowledge are described in universal terms as being without limit, as when we say that God is all knowing and almighty : whereas the will, seeing that it is the determining force, cannot cover all things, but only those to which it determines power and knowledge.[10]

Clearly, what is not willed is not actualized. If God's will, then, "cannot cover all things", God's power is not wholly actualized. On the other hand, to deny unactualized potentialities in God, is to deny the argument that God's power, unlike his will, is "without limit". In other words, two alternative relations between God's will and power are possible : (1) to protect the concept *actus purus*, it can be maintained that the extent of divine power is identical with the determination of God's will. Since what can be willed is, by the nature of the case, limited (there are mutually incompatible possibilities), God's power cannot be "without limit"; (2) to protect the divine omnipotence, it could be maintained that God's power extends beyond his will. The latter is, of course, Aquinas' position. For example, Aquinas holds that God could have created a better universe than that which actually exists.[11] But either the *absurdum*

[9] C. G. II, 25.2.

[10] De Pot., 1.7.

[11] Summa Ia, 25.6; De Pot., 3.16c. Nevertheless, in the Contra Gentiles, Aquinas reasons that God is the highest good whose will "can will nothing except

must then be held that no matter how God acts, he remains in the exact same state of being, i.e., 'doing' is assumed as irrelevant to 'being', or potentiality must be admitted into deity on the ground that God could have willed and acted other than he did and therefore his state of being, in its details, could have been different from what it is.

My argument, then, is that three errors flaw Aquinas' doctrine of divine omnipotence and prevent his thought from correcting itself; namely, (1) the unquestioned assumption that perfection excludes passivity, (2) the refusal to consider values that are unique to the possession of passive power, (3) the failure to think through the analysis of divine power to that point where logic implies the presence of passive power in deity. I turn now to the specifics of Aquinas' doctrine to substantiate these points in detail.

A threefold character informs Aquinas' idea of God's power : its universality, its uniqueness, its absoluteness. It is universal in that it extends to all things with which the notion of being is not incompatible.[12] It is unique in that it is creative : God alone has the power to create being, as such, out of nothing.[13] It is absolute (where absolute means complete and non-relative), in that no effect lies beyond God's power; [14] "God is able to do everything whatsoever that lies within the potency of the created being".[15]

It is evident that the sheer uniqueness of God's power depends upon the absolute quality of that power, but notice that the universality of divine power is neither dependent upon, nor equivalent in meaning to, the absoluteness of power. I would like to argue that the universality of God's power is the fundamental notion because absolute power presupposes the universal extension of power, while the reverse is not true. That is, the notion that God's power reaches to all things does not require the total efficaciousness of that power. On the other hand, the assertion of absolute power threatens to leave no logical room for the notion of real creaturely power. Similarly the notion of the absolute uniquesness of divine creativity explicitly disallows the notion of local creativity.[16] Thus,

---

by willing itself ... (and therefore that will) cannot will evil". C. G. II, 92.2-5.

[12] C. G. II, 22.1-4.

[13] C. G. II, 21.4.

[14] C. G. II, 22.7-8.

[15] C. G. II, 22.5.

[16] C. G. II, 21.

the problematic in Aquinas' idea of God's power arises not from the fundamental notion of universal power but from the refining of that basic notion to include absolute and uniquely creative power.

The rejection of local creativity follows quite logically from the absolute quality of divine power. If creatures have the power to create or to add to being, then divine power would be qualified and God would not be absolute in power. Thus, the issue of local creativity cannot arise with any force in Thomas' scheme as long as the notion of divine absolute power is considered a cogent notion. What is crucial for Aquinas is the successful working out of a doctrine of real creaturely power within the doctrine of God's absolute power. His task is to set forth a doctrine of finite power that affirms its reality, but not its creativity.

The duality of Thomas' intention is clear. "God works in every natural thing" he holds "not as though the natural thing were altogether inert, but because God works in both nature and will when they work".[17] Thus, the creatures are not mere "inert" instruments of the divine will, but maintain some real activity, some real power for themselves. Yet the intention to maintain the absoluteness of God's power is also clear : "God works... when they work". This double intention places Aquinas at a methodological crossroads; that is, two polar methods are possible to meet his task. The first is an empirical analysis of local activity and power where the key problem lies in determining how and to what extent God's power is an ingredient in every creaturely act; the second is a rational analysis deducing the extent of divine power from God's absoluteness or perfection where the key problem is how and to what extent local power is an ingredient in the creature's act. The issue here is whether knowledge of creaturely power takes its point of departure in the knowledge of sensibles or from the knowledge of already established concepts of God. To argue that, in this case, the method of approach is indifferent to the outcome, simply presupposes the compatibility between the notion of divine absolute power and real creaturely power. This presupposition, however, is the real issue, for if the two notions fail to make sense together, then one or the other, depending on the methodology elected, will be radically qualified in the process of relating them.

Aquinas' method is the deductive one. As Thomas Gilby demon-

[17] De Pot., 3.7.

strates, in an appendix to the new English translation of the *Summa*,[18] the way in which the divine power is held to bear upon the activity of a creaturely power has its ground in the nature of deity that emerges from the proofs of God's existence. Gilby details the correspondence between the proofs and the ways in which primary power relates to secondary power. For our own purposes, it will be sufficient to note the general lines of his argument.

Gilby argues that Aquinas sees four ways in which the divine first cause bears upon the action of a secondary cause; namely, as providing the being of the causal agent, preserving it, moving the power of the agent to act, and as entering into the action itself as principal agent.[19] That no creature can provide or preserve its own power to be is at the very heart of the proofs which take their force from the notion that no created cause is source of its own existence or its own activity. For example, the explicit outcome of the fourth proof, which holds that the being of creatures is being by participation, is that creaturely activity is always and necessarily dependent upon a first principle and cause of all activity.[20] The notion that it is God's power which moves the local power to act finds its root in the proof from motion, which is concerned not so much with God's temporal priority, as with His ontological priority to any local agent's motion. Thus, every local act presupposes the divine pre-motion as, Aquinas suggests analogously, a knife's cutting presupposes the "fact that (someone) applies the sharpness of the knife to cutting by moving it to act".[21] Finally, Aquinas' argument that God enters into the action " as a principal agent causes the action of its instrument" [22] finds it ground and meaning in the proof from causality. The notion here is that as an instrument requires an agent to move it to an effect beyond its own proper power to produce, so God, as the metaphysical first cause of every being, enters into every action to produce what is beyond the proper power of every creaturely cause; namely, the being of the effect or accident.

The obvious methodological weakness in deducing the character

---

[18] Thomas Gilby, "appendix 3", Vol. 2 in St. Thomas Aquinas, Summa Theologia, ed. and E.T. Thomas Gilby O. P., (London, Eyre and Spottiswoode, 1963), p. 209-210.

[19] Summa I, 105.5; De Pot. 3.7.

[20] For the proofs, see Summa Ia, 2-3.

[21] De Pot., 3.7.

[22] De Pot., 3.7.

of divine activity from the proofs is of course the questionable status of the proofs.[23] Yet it must be added that this criticism, in itself, is not fatal if the metaphysic that emerges from the proofs achieves an inner coherence and an adequacy to the facts of our secular, religious and moral experience. Thus, granting Aquinas his methodology, our own task is to inquire into his understanding of the nature and role of the secondary cause, judging it by the criteria of adequacy to experience and inner consistency.

We can begin with the following key texts :

it (the secondary cause) is the cause of the action precisely inasmuch as this latter is this individual action.[24]

It (the secondary cause) is the cause of the becoming of the effect and not directly of its being.[25]

The action of a corporeal agent does not extend beyond the limits of motion and therefore it is the instrument of the primal agent in the educing of forms from the potentiality of matter, which is accomplished through motion.[26]

The initial text asserts the particularity of every action so that in any given series of natural events, each particular event can be assigned its particular, local cause. Aquinas' thrust here is to affirm the possibility of a scientific explanation of natural phenomena within a theology of the absolute. Though God wills all things, and his will is uncaused, nevertheless the expression of that will is through concrete secondary causes.[27] Thus, a secondary cause is real in the sense that it is the necessary locus of local action.

The next two texts go more to the heart of the matter, for in them Thomas seeks a role for secondary causes midway between that of adding to the sum of created being – which God alone can do – and leaving created being precisely as it is – which would simply mean that a secondary cause does nothing at all. The solution draws upon two Aristotelian distinctions; that between form and matter, and that between actuality and potentiality. Thus God's eternal will determines what will be, but the forms of future things are only potentially present, they lack material actualization. The role of the

---

[23] For a recent collection of arguments regarding the validity of the proofs, see John Hick, ed., *The Existence of God*, (New York : Macmillan, 1964).

[24] De Pot., 3.7.

[25] Summa Ia, 104.1.

[26] De Pot., 5.1.

[27] Summa Ia, 19.5.

secondary cause is, through local motion, to effect the change from the potency of matter to the actuality of being, and thereby to assist in the realization of the possibilities of the universe. In this sense, secondary powers are God's necessary instruments for his creative will, and in this way, Aquinas can attribute to the creation a contributory role in the acquiring of its own proper realization.

Now this analysis of the process of actualization bristles with philosophic problems. For example, it assumes matter as pure potency, whereas any bit of matter is inconceivable unless it has some form; it assumes that the material universe and its present type of order is a fully articulated and eternally formed system,[28] thereby providing inadequate room for the evolution of matter. Nevertheless, for the present at least, my concern is to stay within Thomas' system to determine the nature of the power he attributes to creatures and the consistency of his thought in this regard.

First of all, the contributing, or real active, role of the secondary cause is limited to that of supplying the motion required to effect the change, in a universe of becoming, from potentiality to actuality. However, the force of assigning even this limited role is mitigated somewhat by the Thomist principle – stemming from the proofs – that God's motion is ontologically prior and absolute in relation to creaturely motion.[29] What this means is that a secondary cause in itself neither reduces itself from potentiality to act, nor moves itself to cause anything. The reason for this is that the individuality of the effect is still 'being', and, therefore, depends for its actualization upon the first cause. Thus, creaturely power can assume the active role Thomas assigns to it only under the influence of the primary power which applies it to its act. In the final analysis, then, all things act in the power of God; no creaturely activity escapes the pervasive possession of the divine cause which "is the cause of action in every created agent".[30]

Nevertheless, even within this stress upon divine power, Thomas works out a doctrine of the integrity and responsible causality of the secondary agent. That he effects such a doctrine is one of the marks of his genius, and the extent of his success in doing so is

[28] De Pot. 3.4.

[29] Cf. also De Pot., 3.7, "The will of God which is the origin of all natural movement precedes the operation of nature, so that its operation is presupposed in every operation of nature".

[30] Summa Ia, 105.5.

crucial to the viability of his doctrine of divine omnipotence. The main lines of the argument are brilliant and brief. Secondary causes are radically subordinate to the divine cause. Nevertheless they are 'real' in that divine power does not override or obliterate a secondary cause's integrity or inner principles of action. This is because the permanent possession of a secondary cause by a first cause is internal and therefore works within the forms and actions of each individual secondary cause. For example, the will, which is the determining seat of creaturely action, is moved subjectively, interiorly, by God, without doing any violence to its natural inclination.[31] Thus, by quite explicitly eschewing the notion that divine activity is constituted by outside interference or external compulsion,[32] Aquinas can grant to created being no immunity from divine causality and yet maintain the minimal conditions for responsible creaturely causality. Further, Aquinas extends this analysis not only to the natural actions of all creatures, but to the free actions of man. Thus he writes :

Our free will is the cause of its act, but it does not of necessity have to be the first cause of its act. God is the first cause, who moves both natural and voluntary causes. And just as by moving natural causes He does not prevent their acts from being natural, so by moving voluntary causes He does not deprive their actions of being voluntary, but rather is He the cause of this very being in them; for He operates in each thing according to its own nature that He has given it.[33]

The upshot of the Thomist solution is this : every creaturely act issues from the divine pre-motion, but secondary causality is real, or contributary to the definiteness of the universe, because God acts only through the natural structures of His creation by subjectively determining their own self-determination. Where the natural structure involved is that of the "free will", that structure remains intact and unviolated by divine causality. The free will consciously determines itself to act, in the sense that its act is not simply the outcome of either its inner nature or external circumstances, or a combination of the two. Divine causality, however, lies behind even the mode of freedom itself in that the freely determined act finds its origin in God's eternal pre-motion.

Two related question emerge from this analysis. The first is whether

[31] Summa Ia, 105.4 and 111.2.
[32] Summa Ia, I, II, 6.4, 9.4 and 6.
[33] Summa Ia, 83.1.

a creaturely power is real or a creaturely act is freely determined where no creaturely effect escapes the eternal will and causative power of the divine being. The second question concerns Aquinas' understanding of creaturely freedom as the absence of coercion or constraint in the determination to act and in the act itself; can such a definition maintain its integrity within his own system? [34]

An analysis of the following will open up these questions :

These two statements are not incompatible : God wills to save this individual and he can be damned. But these two statements are incompatible : God wills this one to be saved and the same one is damned. [35]

The key to understanding Aquinas here lies in bearing in mind and applying the distinction he draws between absolute necessity and necessity of supposition. Thus the first statement, that an individual can be damned whom God wills to save, refers to the general possibility of damnation. That is, there is nothing in either God or man that requires by absolute necessity either the salvation or damnation of any individual. Considered abstractly, then, man's nature is free, his power is real, his destiny is open, "he can be damned". On the other hand, according to the necessity of supposition, the concrete determination of God, which has no cause other than the divine will, is subject to neither change nor failure. Therefore, what God concretely wills, necessarily (by supposition) happens, so that it is impossible that "God wills this one to be saved and the same one is damned". Thus, Aquinas affirms the individual's freedom and power (to final self-determination) in the abstract, and divine absoluteness of power (to determine the final determination of other selves) in the concrete.

This analysis, if it is correct, throws light on the question regarding the metaphysical identity of the agent of the creature's power and, in the case of man, of his freedom. The structure of a creature is a structure of local power, the structure of man is a structure of local freedom, but the agent that wills the concrete determination of that power, that is, the agent that effects the move from this particular

[34] (I avoid here the thorny issue as to whether or not Aquinas affirms the capacity of creaturely power to resist cooperation with the divine action. On the one hand we have : "the act of resisting is incompossible with the efficacy of the divine motion". Summa I, II 10, 4; on the other hand there is much ambiguity on this issue; cf. Summa Ia, 19.8, 105.4, C. G. III 88-90; De Malo 6.1).

[35] St. Thomas Aquinas, Truth, E.T.R. Mulligan, J. McGlynn, R. Schmidt, (Chicago : H. Regnery and Company, 1952-54), 23.5.

potential power to that particular actual power is God. Similarly, God is the agent who has freely determined the open destiny of man. From the creature's perspective his power is real in that he also contributes to the making (or wreckage) of the universe, but it is God who effectuates the concrete uses of power. From man's perspective, his freedom is real in that the determination of his destiny is open, but the freedom to concretely determine that destiny belongs not to man, but to God. What the dimension of power and freedom in the creature means, then, is that God has the power and freedom to act upon the world, through the structures of the world, according to his own will. Thus the world even in part does not determinatively set its own definiteness; its openness to alternative states of definiteness, which is the structure of its power and freedom, is an openness to God's ultimate and eternal determination.

The ontological base for this doctrine of God's power and freedom is, of course, the "a se" notion of God. Divine being alone, existing sheerly out of itself and possessing its own principle of action, has its being in absolute independence of what its creativity throws up.[36] In stark contrast is the absolute dependence of created being upon deity for both its being and activity. Local power then is radically secondary power; in the power to be and the power to act, it remains absolutely dependent upon God. Similarly, local freedom is radically secondary freedom, not only in the sense that it is dependent upon God for the mode of freedom itself, but in that the local free act is, ultimately, transparent not to the creature's freedom, but to God's freedom to act according to his will. The principles of Thomism are such that no aspect or accident of non-self-existent being can realize its determination except by reason of the eternal determining act of self-existent being.

---

[36] Cf. Gilson, *The Spirit of Medieval Philosophy*, p. 103 : "For when it is the sovereign good that acts then we have the unique case in which the sole possible end of the act is self-communication. Beings always strive more or less to realize themselves; Being, since He is already fully realized, can act only to give".

CHAPTER V

POWER AND CREATIVITY — PART II

Aquinas conceives of freedom as the harmony of will and act, and thereby seeks to reconcile to each other the idea of divine absolute power and human freedom. Consider the argument : God's power is absolute in so far as his power is at the base of the acts of the free self; the acts of the self are free, or self-determined, in so far as God's power works internally through the structure of the will so that there is no conflict between the act of the self and the will of the self. In other words, a free act is constituted by the assent of the will to the act of the self, even though both the power to will and the power to act find their origin in God's will and power. Thus, the concept of divine omnipotence does not divest man of his freedom to act upon his will but it does divest the idea of freedom of the dimension of openness to the future or real alternative possibility. For Aquinas, creaturely freedom involves only the category of assent; the category of real choice or real alternative belongs within the mystery of God's eternity.

Similarly, an analysis of Aquinas' argument for the reality of creaturely power reveals a qualification of the idea of real power. By conceiving of the power of the secondary cause as the power to effect change, rather than create new being, Aquinas has sought to affirm real creaturely power without compromising the absolute quality of God's power. To accomplish this aim, he has had to divest the idea of real power of all notion of creativity, novelty and ontological additiveness. Real power, in the creaturely case, involves, for Aquinas, neither novel contribution to being nor addition to reality itself. In Aquinas' schema, the endless multiplication of beings and their acts adds nothing to being, it only adds more beings to the creation.[1]

---

[1] C. G. I, 75.3. Cf. also J. Maritain, *Degrees of Knowledge*, E. T., G. Phelan (New York : Scribner's, 1959), p. 234.

In a word, the power of created being is an ontologically useless power.

Aquinas' doctrine of omnipotence, then, can tolerate only a restricted definition of creaturely freedom and cannot tolerate at all the dimension of ontological creativity within the concept of creaturely power. My argument is that this restrictive definition of freedom and this absolute denial of creaturely creativity raise sufficient logical, moral, and religious problems to bring the doctrine of divine omnipotence into serious question.

The logical difficulties that arise out of Aquinas' understanding of the relation of divine to secondary power have to do with the social nature of power and the concept of time. Power involves the power to act and this includes that action by which we maintain our existence or being. It is then logically impossible for a creature to exist without any inherent power for a completely powerless being simply could not have being. This suggests that the character of our world is that of a plurality or society of mutually limiting powers. Aquinas' position is that all creatures do indeed have power but that there is no power that is not ultimately the power of God. Behind this position lies the argument for God's ontological priority to each creature's act; that is, every creaturely motion presupposes the divine pre-motion. Aquinas is certainly correct in asserting the world's dependence upon God – no theology could do less than this. His difficulty arises out of his insistence that God's power is absolute and primary, thus wrenching the concept of power out of the social context which it requires to gain logical coherence. The point is that given the dynamic conception of God there cannot be any talk about an absolute ontological priority, for it is as true to say that every creaturely motion presupposes the divine pre-motion as it is to say that the divine pre-motion presupposes real creaturely power. In other words, the logical outcome of an analysis of power is an antinomy which is antithetical to a view of deity as the ultimate possessor of all power.

Further, the logic of omnipotence, in affirming creativity as a property unique to divine power, threatens to empty the concept of time of any meaningful content. Aquinas defines creativity as "an active power whereby things are brought into being (requiring) no pre-existing matter or previous agency".[2] Further, creativity does not presuppose any prior cause but is itself such a cause.[3] Aquinas

---

[2] De Pot., 3.4.
[3] Summa Ia, 65.3; C. G. II, 21.

quite correctly sees that to allow creativity to creaturely beings is to allow for the ongoing creativity of Being. Since God is Being, absolute in power and without passivity or potentiality, He alone can be creative. Further, creative power must be understood under the category of the eternal rather than the temporal in order to avoid admitting potentiality into Being. Thus, in the end, creativity is limited to an act encompassing all time in the eternal now rather than a succession of acts throughout time. What Thomas has done here is to so define creativity as to confine it to a mode of being which is *a se, actus purus*, absolute, non-temporal, etc.

The question I wish to raise here is the effect upon the concept of time in a thought system which denies creativity to those entities involved in the ongoingness of things. The only answer is that from the perspective of God's will and power, time is the sequential rehappening of what happens simultaneously in eternity.[4] From the creaturely perspective, temporal becomingness is real, that is, to us, there is a future time which is not yet. This perspective, however, is an illusion due to the inherent ignorance of the temporal mode of being which can know things only in succession rather than in simultaneity. Thus, the logic of Aquinas' position leads to the conclusion that nothing ever really becomes, rather what we call becomingness is merely the movement from what is eternally true to its brief embodiment in the temporal world.[5] In other words, we can speak of the reality of becoming, only if we mean that things lacked the definiteness of being prior to their temporal occurrence. But even here, since God eternally knows and creates things in their definiteness, then nothing is non-existent, and the concept of time is divested of the dimension of becomingness.[6]

---

[4] Strictly speaking, there is, in this view, no divine perspective upon time. The distinction between the actual and the "not yet" actual does not arise for God. As God's power excludes passivity, so his mode of Knowing excludes succession; i.e., God does not know in terms of past, present and futures. It would be naive, for example, to ask whether God Knows about a loss that I have experienced at the moment that I have experienced it. God Knows about my loss from eternity; He does not Know "when" it happens. In other words, what God Knows as actual, He Knows as part of His eternity, not as part of our temporality.

[5] Again, notice the implicit shift to an idealist metaphysic where Aquinas concerns himself with "the divine case".

[6] These strains in Aquinas' thought have been uncovered before, cf. Patterson, *The Concept of God in the Philosophy of Aquinas*, pp. 443 ff.; Charles Hartshorne,

Thomas, of course, sought to hold together both the reality of a world of becoming and God's eternal mode of being and creating. But he runs into difficulty because he is beset by (logically) irreconcileable notions; for example, that things become (for man), that things are (for God); that the character of future things lacks definiteness (for man), that no things lack definiteness (for God). From this situation we either move to the idea of a special logic in the divine case – which would provide us with the philosophical justification for the affirmation of opposing statements [7] – or we must make some hard choices. Either nothing becomes or creativity characterizes the temporal world (i.e., creatures participate in adding to the determinativeness of being). Either the definiteness of the world is given in a once-for-all eternity, or new definiteness is added to being from time to time. Either reality disappears into the divine being or creatures have a role in determining reality. Even more, either freedom does not involve alternative possibility or the affirmation of freedom requires the creative participation of temporal being in the additiveness of the world.

Where one comes down, then, in this either – or situation depends upon the position taken in respect to the character of the actuality of this world. If the experience of the becomingness of things is held onto as a blunt fact of experience then it follows that no event achieves actual definiteness until it occurs in time. If this is the character of things, then we live in a world in which no event in its full definiteness is decided until it achieves temporal actualization. Further, if the very analysis of power, requires for its coherence a plurality of powers, then the notion of a uniquely creative power underlying all acts of power simply fails to make sense. It would seem that we must affirm, in principle, a plurality of powers and decisions as constitutive in the creation of any actual existent being or event. In sum it is not simply a matter of desiring to limit divine power in order to save man from the thought of ontological uselessness, for unless we limit divine power the truth of the way in which we experience and know the world becomes undermined and our

----

Beyond Humanism, (Chicago : Willett, Clark and Company, 1937), pp. 129 ff.; and Hartshorne, *The Logic of Perfection*, pp. 165 ff.

[7] The difficulty involved in developing and applying to the doctrine of God a logic of the absolute or of the infinite, is that it would be purely rationalistic or deductive in character, and would allow for no empirical checks.

logical mode of reasoning about the nature of things becomes questionable. I turn now to the moral argument against the concept of omnipotence.

The nagging inadequacy of the concept of omnipotence to the fact of evil is, of course, the perennial problem and scandal of orthodoxy. Anthony Flew's recent, thorough and devastating critique of orthodoxy on this point [8] is sufficiently well known so as not to warrant any repetition in detail here. The burden of his argument, namely, that there is no contradiction involved in God so determining people that they always freely choose the right, is fatal to the orthodox theodicy which holds that evil is the price of human freedom. From the perspective of my own argument, the significant point is that Thomas' mode of resolving God's absolute causality with the affirmation of human freedom simply substantiates the very basis for Flew's argument that evil in the world destroys theism.

Both Flew and Thomas agree that freedom means inner determination or the absence of constraint upon the will. Further, both thinkers agree that divine omnipotence allows for God's acting upon man so as to freely determine man to do what God wills him to do. Flew concludes from this that such definitions of human freedom and divine power places upon deity full responsibility for all that happens.[9] His most pointed argument is that the attempt to shift the responsibility for evil to man's free acts can only raise the suspicion that the notion of an all-powerful, all-good, creator God is a logically vicious concept.[10]

Flew's thesis that evil in the world destroys the cogency of the notion of God depends upon two interrelated assumptions : that omnipotence means that there is no power that is not the power of God; that the interior act of will delimits the meaning of human freedom. Given these assumptions and definitions the issue here is not whether human freedom is logically compatible with divine omnipotence. One need not argue with Garrigou-Lagrange's statement that no one "could demonstrate that there is any contradiction in maintaining that the creator of the free will, who is more intimately

---

[8] Anthony Flew, "*Divine Omnipotence and Human Freedom*", in Anthony Flew and Alistair MacIntyre eds., *New Essays in Philosophical Theology*, (London : Student Christian Movement Press, 1955), pp. 144-169.

[9] *Ibid.*, p. 167.

[10] *Ibid.*, p. 165.

associated with the will than freedom itself is, can infallibly move the will to determine itself freely to act".[11] Rather, what must be argued is whether, in fact, Aquinas' mode of overcoming the logical tension between the concept of human freedom and divine power avoids placing the responsibility for evil upon God. Aquinas desired to affirm man's responsibility for those human choices involving both evil intention and outcome.[12] The issue here is whether he can have it both ways. Can he hold that "in no way can God fail",[13] and yet suggest that human evil prevents God from producing a perfect world? If human evil hinders the achievement of any divine value then it is an example of a creaturely activity which limits God's power. On the other hand, to argue that creaturely activity does not limit divine power, is to shift the responsibility for evil activity from man to God.

Clearly the question is how to avoid vitiating the concept of divine goodness within the context of the problem of evil. To do so it is necessary not only to assert, as Thomas does, the division of responsibility for whatever is, but to realize that the idea of division of responsibility loses its cogency unless it is also understood that it implies division of power. The extent and character of divine power must then be viewed within the social dimension in which all power is found; that is, we never find power alone but rather find one power acting upon and reacting to other powers. From this perspective it can make no sense to hold that God possesses all the active power there is, or that there is no active power that is not absolutely dependent upon divine power. Such assertions move towards obscurantism because they imply that power, in the divine case, stands outside the social context in which the concept power gains its meaning and where the act of power is realized.[14]

Hartshorne, of course, has been urging us for many years to think of divine power as supremely maximal power. In this view, God possesses all the power that a single being can possess, but He cannot possess the power which is inherent in other things by the mere fact of their existence. God's power then is maximal, it is supreme; but where even the maximal case of power must be social that power

[11] R. Garrigou-Lagrange, *God, His Existence and His Nature*, E.T. Dom. Bede Rose (St. Louis, Mo., and London : B. Herder Book Co., 1955), p. 76.
[12] Summa Ia, 49.2; C. G. III, 10.
[13] C. G. II 25.6.
[14] Cf. the argument above.

must take account of the power of others. This means that God's power to achieve his ends, both ultimate and penultimate, is limited by creaturely powers. It also means that worldly entities are involved in the creative actualization of possibilities that excludes the concept of an "eternal now" but not the concept of an eternal envisionment of formal possibilities. Given this perspective, then, God's supreme or maximal power can be understood as presenting to every worldly occasion a relevant possibility for realization and, by holding before the world a universal and stable order, setting appropriate limits to creaturely self-determination. Thus, God's power acts as the universal limit to the creatures' powers, and in this sense God's power (partially, but maximally) determines the outcomes of events. In reference to the traditional notion of omnipotence, the crucial point is that it is logically impossible for an object of awareness, even a supreme and universal object, to dictate to a subject of awareness any precise response where in any given case a broad range of responses is possible.[15] In sum, the notion of supreme, maximal and even universal power has meaning only within a structure of understanding which allows for partial self-determination on the part of finite and local agents. Thus, the beginnings of a theological solution to the problem of evil is laid : [16] God's goodness remains absolute, his power to achieve goodness in the creation is limited by the morally ambiguous powers of the creatures. From Aquinas' point of view, however, this basis for a solution to the problem of God raised by the fact of evil is unacceptable because it cuts across two basic and interrelated doctrines in his thought; namely, the purely active character of God and the strictly non-creative character of the creature.

The idea of God in Aquinas' thought is that of a sheerly active being in whom no potentiality or possibility for change or determination from other beings are admitted. Thus, though the end of God's activity is God's goodness, God does not act to realize or intensify his goodness, for it is (eternally) perfect and complete, nor does he act in order to possess goodness, for his being is identical

---

[15] Cf. Hartshorne, *The Divine Relativity*, pp. 139 ff., and *The Logic of Perfection*, pp. 163 ff.

[16] The immediate religious objection to such a beginning is that it would not allow for a final necessary conquest of evil. I consider this a serious objection, and the whole of Chapter VIII, below, is devoted to answering it.

with goodness. For Aquinas, then, God acts not to achieve the end of goodness, but to produce effects which will participate in that goodness. According to this concept of God, no action, neither a divine nor a creaturely one, can affect God's being (eg., his goodness); God cannot be moved, changed, or suffer failure (failure implies privation, and, therefore, potentiality); he cannot repent, or be angry, or sorrow.[17] Thus, the purely active God is neither included in nor dependent upon the ordered structure and process of the universe. Indeed since the creator is not affected by the activity or power of the creature, the character of the relation of creator to creature itself become problematical. Thomas' solution here is to hold that the creator's relation to the creature is purely a logical conception rather than a real (i.e. affecting) one.[18]

To admit a doctrine of partial self-determination of local agents is fatal to the notion of God as absolute cause and as *actus purus*. For to hold that the final determination of an historical event lies in part with the entities involved in the event means that events have real alternatives so that in its details the future is radically unknown. This means that historical details enter into the divine experience and contribute to the divine reality only as these details occur in their temporal succession.

Still, the admission of an element of creaturely self-determination need not threaten the concept of God as creator and cause of all things; God can be conceived as the being uniquely and universally necessary for the creatures self-determining acts. What it does preclude is the concept of God as absolute or sheer cause in that it insists that we think of God as "affected by" as well as "cause of" when we consider God's relation to other beings. To put it another way, God, in the view suggested by Hartshorne, remains the supreme influence in that his influence is necessary and universal; but he must also be conceived as universally influenced, for in conceiving of divinity as supreme being it is just as necessary to hold that nothing escapes the supreme universal sensitivity as to hold that nothing escapes the supreme universal causality. The point to note here is that the affirmation of supreme sensitivity to the happenings of the world does not entail a threat to the (immutable) metaphysical identity of being which marks divinity as divinity. God remains

---

[17] C. G. II, 25; Summa Ia, 25.3.
[18] Summa Ia, 13.7; De Pot. 3.3.

supremely loving, righteous, holy, wise etc., and no creaturely act of power can alter this. What does change in God is his total value experience, which is cumulative rather than simultaneously whole, and his action in relation to the creatures, which is responsive to the temporal situation thrown up by the world rather than eternally present. Thus, not only logical but real relations exist between creator and creature, not only active power but passive power must be attributed to deity and finally not only an eternal aspect of being but a termporal aspect of being describe the divine existence. To admit this much inevitably draws the discussion into the second point rejected by Aquinas; namely, the creativity of the creature. The reason for this is that to affirm the creature's contribution to the details and value of reality is precisely to affirm what is meant by the creativity of the creatures. It is necessary then to turn once more, this time in greater depth, to an examination of the whole issue of creativity.

Aquinas rightly understood that the assertion of the creativity of the creature would entail the notions of the ongoing creativity of Being and of the potentiality of deity. The function of the doctrine that God alone is creative [19] is precisely to preclude these notions. Thomas' rejection of the possibility of creaturely creativity is clear and uncompromising; a creature can neither create by its own power nor create "ministerially as an instrument".[20] To maintain this view, Thomas limited the category of creativity to the act of creation, and he understood the creation as a once-for-all fully articulated system and eternally formed event requiring neither matter nor any existing agency other than deity.[21] Thus, from the perspective of the creature, a creative act is a mystery, utterly denied to him and therefore utterly remote from any possible creaturely experience.

My argument is that the denial of creativity is fatal to the idea of moral freedom, and consequently of moral responsibility. Moral freedom and responsibility involve a leap beyond the necessary or eternally given; the morally free act in any situation assumes growth, unpredictable in its concreteness. In this sense, a moral act brings something (concretely) new into actual existence; new not only for the creature, but for God as well. Thus, the idea of moral freedom converges with the idea of creativity so that the meaning

[19] C. G. II 17.21; Summa Ia, 65.3.
[20] De Pot. 3.4.
[21] De Pot. 3.4; see Gilson, *The Spirit of Medieval Philosophy*, p. 161.

of moral freedom attains its cogency only when thought together with the idea of creativity.[22] It is this aspect of the analysis of moral freedom that is refused recognition by Aquinas, and this refusal threatens his doctrine of human freedom and divine omnipotence with the charge of obscurantism.[23]

Finally, I turn to the religious problems that beset Aquinas' doctrine of omnipotence. There are two related ones; namely, man's ontological futility and God's ontological neutrality.

Aquinas' basic presupposition is that God in himself is absolute perfection and that an increase in absolute perfection is logically absurd. Consequently, God in his inner life or in his quality of being, would be none the less infinitely good, wise and rich in being even without the creation. God, Aquinas holds, "necessarily wills himself to be, to be good, and to be happy."[24] Further, as far as the richness and value of his experience is concerned, God's being is utterly indifferent or neutral to the creatures' loving or hating, rejoicing or suffering, praying or damning, constructing or destroying, etc... For Aquinas, "God can neither repent, nor be angry or sorrowful, because all these things bespeak passion or defect".[25] Thus, the refusal to allow passive power as a property of deity inevitably leads to the conclusion that the quality of God's being is indifferent to the quality of creaturely activity. Since God's being contains the being of the world in the eternal moment, the creature's temporal activity is, ontologically speaking, useless and futile.[26]

Aquinas, then, has so conceived the character of divine power as to deny the possibility of God's receiving anything from the world. For Aquinas, God's relation to the world is logical or external;

---

[22] Bergson deserves the credit for first seeing with remarkable clarity the connection between the moral and the creative act. Cf. Henri Bergson, *Creative Evolution*, E.T. Arthur Mitchell, (New York : Modern Library, 1944), pp. 263-4, 271-2.

[23] As is candidly admitted by Garrigou-Lagrange, *God, His Existence and His Nature*, p. 89.

[24] C. G. II 25.21.

[25] C. G. II 25.9.

[26] This is not simply a "Protestant" interpretation; cf. Gilson, *The Christian Philosophy of St. Thomas Aquinas*, p. 337; Maritain, *Degrees of Knowledge*, p. 234; Garrigou-Lagrange, *God, His Existence and Nature*, pp. 100-101. Gilson, in the above reference, goes so far as to admit that "what or whether we pray makes little difference to God's action, being, joy etc.". Cf. also Summa II, II 2.2 and 83.2.

therefore, by definition, God's being as being is absolutely neutral between any and all relational alternatives. In other words, God's being is utterly indifferent to what is thrown up by the world. This notion of the ontological neutrality of a God who as being is absolutely indifferent to the state of our being, strains hard against the Biblical-religious picture of an historically active Yahweh responsively and sympathetically relating to a particular people as they seek to understand who they are and whom they are called upon to become. Such a strain exists because two different ideas of divine being are at issue : that of a sheerly independent and complete being unqualified by relations, and that of a being qualified and conditioned by concrete social relations, and absolute (or complete and unchanging) only in the abstract form of the integrity of his faithfulness to and ultimate aim for his people. My own feeling is that there is no way of mediating these two notions of divine being; the issue for Christian doctrine is which (if either) notion of deity is required by a religion which has as its central symbol God-incarnate hanging on the cross in suffering love.

Aquinas' genius lay in the thoroughness of his attempt to synthesize Aristotle's notion of the deity of God as sheer completeness of being with the Biblical notion of a dynamic God sympathetically uniting Himself to His creation. The success of this attempt hinged on whether Thomas could consistently think through the notion of a God who cares for the world with the notion of a God who lacks the power to be affected by it (i.e., lacks passive power). Aquinas sought to accomplish this aim by forcing divine love into the mold of self-interest; that is, in the divine case, Aquinas removed love from a relational or social structure, and placed it in a radically atomistic one. In other words, he tried to give love a meaning outside a mutually qualifying structure.[27] The end result was the affirmation of a loving God within an ontology of indifference. The problem here is whether love of others and ontological indifference to the state of others are mutually compatible possibilities. My own argument is that the concept love loses its meaning unless it is conceptually understood as involving openness to or participation in that which lies beyond the self. Love finds its meaning within an inter-related

---

[27] It can and has been argued that one of the functions of Trinitarian dogma is to establish the social nexus for the divine love without qualifying the "a se" character of God. The issue is whether or not Trinitarian thought itself requires the social nexus of a world. Cf. Chapter VII, below.

social structure, and Thomas' attempt to conceive God as an exception to social existence is fatal to the religious conception of God as love. In a word, it is a religious *absurdum* to speak of a loving God who is unaffected by creaturely suffering, praying, destroying, etc... That Aquinas' synthesis leads to such an *absurdum* can only suggest that an Aristotelian ontology is inadequate to the Christian idea of God.

The sum of the discussion so far is this : working with an Aristotelian ontology, Aquinas has refused to admit passive power into deity, and accepting the corollary of this, he has denied creativity to the creatures. The result for his Christian doctrine of power has been logical, moral and religious *absurdum* of such fundamental importance as to suggest an error in theological methodology. The location of this methodological error is pointed to by the very analysis which disclosed the problem; namely ,Aquinas' assumption that divine being is quite properly an exception in every case to the ontological principles that characterize being in general. This raises the question whether it is possible to conceive of God in such a way that his being can be understood within the categories of the ontological principles. Specifically, can divine power be divine without being absolute?

Hartshorne has argued that a doctrine of divine power can be founded upon the idea of the supremacy of God's power in relation to all the forms of the power of being, and he has worked this out in terms of the absolute adequacy of God's power to cosmic need.[28] In this view God is the supreme exemplar of both the passive and active forms of power. The supporting argument here is that in our own experience passivity or sensitivity to change is not universally considered a defect of being. Contrary to Aquinas' argument [29] what we know about finite life suggests that impassivity rather than being an attribute proper to the highest form of being is, in fact, an attribute distinctive to the lowest forms of being. It is in the lowest forms of life that perfect or pure impassivity is approached; in the higher forms we find increasing sensitivity, passivity and discriminatory responses.[30] To be influenced, in itself, then, is not necessarily a mark of imperfection, though being influenced in a misleading or in a non-discriminating, disproportionate way, might well indicate a mode of imperfect being.

[28] Hartshorne, *The Divine Relativity*, pp. 134-142.
[29] Cf. C. G. II, 25.9.
[30] Hartshorne, *op. cit.*, pp. 105 ff.

Four points here serve to protect the divinity of God's power. First, though the supremacy of divine power can no longer mean that our experiences do not influence God, it can mean that they do not influence Him disproportionately or in the wrong direction. God is here conceived as receiving the activity of the world, but there is the qualification that He receives it in His own way. Secondly, God's responses to the activity of the world are not dictated by the world but are informed ultimately by His own integrity of being and by the unswervingness of His aim for the world. This concept of integrity protects the divine freedom and marks the limits of the passivity of God. God's integrity is His essence or His structure, it is a purely formal aspect of His being and is, therefore, not subject to change; His integrity is His immutability. Thirdly, the supremacy of divine power lies in its universality. God's power extends over all that exists, both in the active sense whereby He is an object of awareness for whatever has being, and in the passive sense whereby His sensitivity or passivity to whatever is alters His "accidental" or "consequential" (non-formal) aspect of being. Thus, this view separates itself from Aquinas in holding that the idea of divine power can be thought through in such a way that the affirmation that God influences all things does not mean that in no ontological sense is God influenced by all things. This aspect of divine power calls for some extended remarks.

The argument of this chapter has been that the difficulties consequent upon Aquinas' doctrine of divine power can be avoided by the ascription of both active and passive power to deity. Aquinas assumed that, in an absolute case, power can compel or, at the least, foreknow, a secondary power's precise manner of response. This assumption is problematical. Divine power can realize itself either through its being an object of awareness, or, in Whitehead's phrase, through acting as a "lure for feeling". The issue then is whether an object of awareness (or a lure for feeling) can compel or guide any given subject to a precise, final response or self-determination. Our own experience suggests that any aware subject, even the highest in the scale of being, lacks the acute sensitivity or delicacy of mental or emotional tone to receive perfectly any given mode of influence. Thus, even if the world were peopled by beings of good will, the limitations of creaturely sensitivity would lead to faulty reception and, consequently, faulty response to the divine will. Since there are an infinite number of ways of missing the (relatively) perfect response, the conclusion is that not even a supreme being can have the power to compel or foreknow any given response.[31] On the other hand, in so far as the creatures' activities are necessarily partially and finally self-determined, they have the possibility to issue in novel occasions.

Thus, unless we are to think of God's will and activity as highly generalized, then it is necessary to understand God as presenting at each moment a partly new ideal, or order of preference, appropriate to the novel occasions. The logic of this analysis of power requires that God relevantly and responsively (to our acts) alter Himself as an object of awareness in order to universally influence and guide the everchanging concrete situations presented to Him by the world. The fourth mode of conceiving the supremacy of divine power requires that we think in terms of maximum social adequacy rather than absoluteness of power. Within a social nexus, as I have argued, the concept of absolute power loses its cogency, so that a social concept of power is needed. A supreme power in a cosmos of many real powers would be a power maximally and eternally adequate to the needs of the cosmos. Such a power, though maximal, is limited : limited in influence, and, consequently, limited in responsibility. Certainly there are problems in a doctrine of a limited God (and I will turn to some of the crucial ones in my last chapter) but such a doctrine has two immediate recommendations for it; it can meet the problem of evil and it avoids the problem of the creatures' ontological uselessness. At the same time, it is possible to conceive God as the essential object of the creatures' experiences in the sense that God can so present Himself to the creature as to weight the possibility of response in the desired direction. Further, in so far as a limited God can be conceived, without contradiction, as laying down the order through which the creatures achieve concrete realization,[32] God can be acknowledged as setting limits (or order) to the activity of the world. The essential point of the argument here is that the character of God's power and influence upon the world is primarily that of persuasion, not compulsion. God controls the world in so far as he established the order for it and has a power maximally adequate to guide it. But God's power and control is

[31] Cf. Hartshorne, *The Divine Relativity*, pp. 138-141, for a fuller discussion on this point.

[32] See the argument for God as a principle of limitation in Whitehead, *Science and the Modern World*, (New York : Mentor, 1948), pp. 156-161.

limited in so far as His maximal influence stops short of the creature's freedom to determine its own concrete response and particular realization of being.

In this view, then, divine power and creaturely freedom are inter-related notions; they must be thought together. God influences us but that influence presupposes our freedom. Here, love, freedom, and creativity converge upon each other, for creativity involves the opening of a being to that which lies beyond its own finite history, and love involves an openness, and freely given response, to that to which a being belongs. But, here too, creativity, freedom, and evil converge, for evil participates in creative power; it adapts its forms, its drive and its energy, but it turns these forms and drives upon their very source and works to destroy the created basis of things. We come, then, full circle, for we approach here a genuine religious ground for Aquinas' rejection of both passivity as a quality of divine power and creativity as a property of creaturely power. The affirmation of divine passivity and creaturely creativity need not threaten the integrity or being of God, but it does threaten the integrity, being, and outcome of the life and the world we know. In the "social" view that I have argued for, we cannot simply look to God's power as providing the kind of absolute security which can assure us that in the end all will have mysteriously worked to have fulfilled God's will or that in the end "all knees shall bend before Jesus Christ". History, in a "social" view, must be under-stood as radically open – open both for God and us. Aquinas' doc-trine of power has, amongst the roots of its inconsistencies, the desire to speak out of the religious sense of ultimate security in divine being. Aquinas' refusal, then, to work out the implications of his thought to their logical, moral and religious *absurdum* has for its ultimate ground a basic facet of our religious experience. Thus, a "social" view of power dissolves some traditional problems that resisted solution within the orthodox concept of deity, but it opens up a problem involving the very heart of the religious life. One of the tasks of a social view of deity, then, is clear : it must make sense of the religious experience of security in spite of pain and evil, and yet still hold on to the notion of the radical openness of the future.

It is certainly true that from the religious perspective the argument of this book becomes so much chaff if a social view of deity is inade-quate to the religious sense of security. Therefore a long final chapter is devoted to arguing the religious adequacy of this view. But before turning to that it is important to see what happens when one raises the question of the adequacy of the concept of simplicity – the concept on which Aquinas philosophically hung the religious experience of absolute security – to the Christian experience of redemption as that experience is theologically expressed in the doctrine of the Trinity.

CHAPTER VI

SIMPLICITY AND PERFECTION

Aquinas' understanding of God is informed throughout by the primacy that he gives to the concept of divine simplicity. The structure of the *Summa* itself reflects this ontological primacy; for example, the "proof" of God's simplicity (in Q3) follows immediately upon the arguments for God. This means that every statement about the quality of divine being (including the Trinitarian statements which begin with Q27) must be brought into line with the notion of simplicity. There is, of course, some Biblical and philosophical justification for this ontological and structural primacy. In the "sh'mai" of the Old Testament, the first affirmation about God is that He "is one God", and in Plotinus' thought the simplicity of divine being is fundamental. Nevertheless the questions I wish to draw attention to concern not the historical roots of the doctrine, but its cogency, not its hoary authority but its uneasy relationship to Trinitarian thought.

There are two texts in the *Summa* which, taken together, get at the underlying meaning of ontological simplicity. The first is found in the prefatory remarks to the discussion of the simplicity of God.

Now, because we cannot know what God is, but rather what He is not, we have no means for considering how God is, but rather how He is not... It can be shown how God is not, by denying of Him whatever is opposed to the idea of Him – viz; composition, motion and the like. Therefore we must discuss His simplicity, whereby we deny composition in Him.[1]

This text points to the negative signification of the concept of simplicity; namely, here the intention is to point to the absence of composition or division in deity. Thus, the content packed into the

---

[1] Summa Ia, 3. preface.

statement "God is simple", is the sum of those statements which
deny the various modes of composite being. Aquinas uncovers six
modes of composition : quantitative parts, matter and form, abstraction and concretion, essence and existence, nature and predicates, subject and accidents.[2] The significant point in Aquinas' argument here concerns not the modes of composition as such but rather the grounds on
which Aquinas bases the denial of the exemplification of these modes
in divine being. In every case, and quite explicitly so, the basis of
his denial depends upon the dictum that there can be no potentiality
in deity.

Simplicity then can be (negatively) defined as the absence of an
ontological structure of change or process; i.e., simplicity means
the absence of novel experiences and acquired perfections. The
reason is that any being which is open to change in any way is by
definition a composite of act and potency (or essence and existence,
or subject and predicate, etc.). It is act in so far as it is something
actual and determinate, it is potency, or relative non-being, in so far
as it is open to change from moment to moment. Aquinas, of course,
rejects any aspect of potentiality in God; God displays no shadow
of change, no alteration, he is simply self-existing and self-explana-
tory "isness". This then is the first way that the concept of simplicity
functions for Aquinas; it serves to protect the notion of God from
the concept of change.

The second text extends the meaning of simplicity beyond the
denial of divisibility or composition.

All created perfections are included in the perfection of being; (for things
are perfect precisely so far as they have being after some fashion. It follows that the perfection of no one thing is wanting to God.)......all things
in a kind of natural unity pre-exist in the cause of all things; thus things
diverse and contradictory in themselves pre-exist in God as one, without
injury to his simplicity.[3]

In this passage the meaning of divine simplicity moves beyond the
negation of division to the overcoming of division. Here, the simplicity of divine being is understood as transcending both oneness
and division, for oneness now includes manifoldness, though it
includes it in a manner other than the ordinary case of manifold
or composite being. In other words, the meaning of simplicity is

---

[2] Summa Ia, 3.1-7.
[3] Summa Ia, 4.2.

much more subtle than mere denial or negation of composition. Aquinas is attempting here to stretch the meaning of simplicity in the divine case so as to mean divisibility overcome rather than divisibility denied. Thus, for Aquinas, God, as the world's cause, includes all created perfections in Himself; things which are diverse pre-exist in God as one, and it is this kind of many-in-oneness that Aquinas seeks to convey by means of the concept simplicity.

Thomas' sophisticated interpretation of simplicity bears fruit for him in establishing a basis for the knowledge of God. For if oneness includes manifoldness, then the oneness of deity becomes the ontological ground of the plurality of the creation; i.e., oneness, in the divine case, is capable of unfolding into the many of the finite world. Further, this understanding of divine oneness lays the basis for the (analogical) knowledge of God. If being composed of really distinct parts is constitutive of creatureliness or caused being, then all objects of human experience are composite, and our conceptions, which spring from our sense knowledge, are correspondingly diverse. The intellect, however, can arrive at knowledge of God through diverse conceptions by understanding that what corresponds to all of them is absolutely one. In other words although, Thomas attributes the mind's apprehension of God in a manifold manner to the weakness or limitations of the human mode of knowing, still the mind can gain true knowledge of God by referring the multiplicity of its conceptions to its own weakness, and by referring unity to the thing understood by the intellect.[4] This does not mean that the intellect can comprehend how power and goodness, for example, can be one; what it does mean is that the logic of affirming an absolutely uncreated cause of being forces the mind to accept the dictum that what is known as diverse in our experience exists as one in the being of God.[5]

The doctrine of divine simplicity then finally focuses on the proposition that a multiplicity of properties and mental conceptions must be thought to fuse at a higher level of being into absolute

[4] C. G. I, 36.2.

[5] Garrigou-Lagrange, in *God, His Existence and Reality*, points up the problem here. "Reason", he holds, "must of necessity come to recognize that in the compossibility and identification of the various attributes, there is involved a philosophic mystery" (p. 200). Interestingly enough, a little further on, he "solves" the mystery : "as they (the attributes) are purified from all imperfection, they tend ... in some way to become identical", (p. 225).

identity. Thus, the doctrine hangs on the possibility that it is meaningful to affirm (1) that at the ground of being, power, goodness, knowledge, love, reason, will, act, etc., are undifferentiated, and (2) that the conscious cause of the plurality of created beings is without a plurality of mental operations and distinctions, i.e., that infinitely complex modes of created being can have their ground in undifferentiated simplicity of being. Thomas is, of course, aware of some of the difficulties in this position, and he seeks to meet them.

We can best see Aquinas' line of defense by carefully analysing his handling of a particular difficult problem in this area. I have in mind the argument against simplicity which is based upon the apparent necessity to distinguish between God's knowledge of Himself and His knowledge of the creation. Thomas states it this way : "if then God understands Himself and something other than Himself as the principal object, He will have several intellectual operations".[6] Also, since God's knowledge includes not only a general but also a concrete knowledge of things, God must know distinctions; that is, he must be aware of both the various modes of being and the concrete diversity within the grades and levels of being.[7] Aquinas sees his problem as finding a place for the distinctions which characterize the content of the divine knowledge, without negating the concept of divine intellect as undifferentiated simplicity.

The key to Aquinas' position on the divine intellect is that God knows other things by knowing himself as the cause.[8] He argues that the likeness of every effect pre-exists in the cause.[9] and therefore when the cause is known, the effect is known.[10] He sums up his argument this way :

By knowing Himself, God knows whatever proceeds from Him immediately. When this is known, God once more knows what proceeds from it immediately; and so on for all intermediate causes down to the last effect.[11]

The basic assumption here is that a cause bears a fundamental likeness to its effect – where fundamental means that the effect can

---

[6] C. G. I, 48.4.
[7] Summa Ia, 15.2; C. G. I 48.7, 51.1.
[8] C. G. I, 49.4.
[9] C. G. I, 49.3.
[10] C. G. I, 50.2.
[11] C. G. I, 50.2. Once again notice how the concept of an absolute God inevitably lends itself, in the working out of its doctrines, to a deterministic schema of things.

be completely accounted for by the cause – otherwise God would be knowing something other than Himself in knowing the effects of His being. Aquinas does not hesitate to make this affirmation : "it belongs to the nature of action that an agent produce its like".[12] More specifically, he states that "the divine essence is the likeness of all things".[13] Thus, the basis for Aquinas' solution lies in his understanding the reality of the world as the unfolding projection of God's (simple) idea of Himself outside of Himself. The key notion here is that the being of this reality, which is external to God, is constituted by the imitation of the idea (in a plurality of modes) which God thinks in thinking Himself. Further, Aquinas argues that there is no distinction in God's thought between the knowledge of the divine essence in itself and the knowledge of that essence as imitable. That is, in the divine case, the movement from knowledge of essence to knowledge of existence does not involve multiple intellectual operations. The rationale, here, is that in perfectly knowing His essence, God would know it under all the modes by which it is knowable, including the mode of imitation.[14]

Aquinas, then, holds that God has ideas within Himself corresponding to each of the beings which make up the universe, but that this plurality of ideas in God does not introduce composition into the divine intellect. Aquinas provides two basic arguments to overcome this apparent conflict. The first is that the plurality of ideas are immediately known, or intuitively contained in God's knowledge of his own eternal mode of being. The second is that God's knowledge of the diversity of the world is not dependent upon or caused by the activity of the world but rather is the cause of the activity of the world. It is precisely for this reason that multiplicity can be held to lie within the unity, for the being of the multiplicity arises sheerly out of the unity. Thus, the keystone of Thomas' thought here is the notion of God as absolute cause; that is, the objects of divine knowledge are dependent upon God for their being, while God's being is totally unaffected by the objects. Thomas, then, can hold that God knows distinctions without affirming distinction in the divine intellect on the ground that the plurality of objects known to God are in a "real" relation to the divine essence, but the divine essence is related only in idea to the objects. In other words, the

12 C. G. I, 29.2.
13 C. G. I, 53.5; cf. also C. G. I, 49.3.
14 C. G. I, 53.5.

distinctions in the divine intellect are only logical distinctions in the divine intellect are only logical distinctions : i.e., distinctions that we make for the sake of saying something about God's being. These distinctions, then, do not really exist in God, for they do not touch the divine essence.

The issue, then, is whether Thomas can make the claim stand that he has avoided the implication of complexity in his defence of the doctrine of simplicity.

Consider first the doctrine of imitation. For Aquinas, the perfections of the world exist originally andeme nintly in the divine being.[15] The thrust of this is not so much that God is the temporal antecedent of the world as it is that he is the ground and sufficient cause of the world. Also, as noted above, Apuinas holds that there is a likeness between ground and consequent, there is a community of nature between that which produces and that which is produced.[16] Since God's "original and eminent" perfection lies in his full actuality of being, everything, in so far as it has being, resembles God. That things fail to resemble God fully is accounted for by their falling short of the fullness of pure being. Now there are certain problems in this way of thinking which become apparent as soon as we raise the question of the character of the definiteness that marks off one existing thing from another. For example, if we followed Aquinas' line of thinking we would say that in so far as a raspberry has a certain degree of being, it resembles God. On the other hand, in so far as it is composed of seedy, slightly bristly, and soft matter, it is subject to decay and loss of being, and fails to resemble God. The difficulty with this kind of thinking is that it is precisely the qualities by which the raspberry fails to resemble God that provide it with thede finiteness which both gives it concrete being and identifies it as a raspberry and not some other mode of being. How then does God gain knowledge of the raspberry? Aquinas had argued that God's knowledge of the many is rooted in their imitation of the one. Therefore, in knowing himself God would know the multiple things in the world in so far as they resemble him. It would seem then that God cannot know the raspberry in its concrete definiteness but can know it simply as undifferentiated being.

[15] Summa Ia, 4.2.
[16] C. G. I, 29.2.

Aquinas deals with this apparent difficulty by reminding us that perfect knowledge of being involves knowledge of all possible modes and grades of being. This resolution, however, bristles with problems. First of all, if all modes of being are somehow contained in God's fullness of being so that the likeness of all things is found in the divine essence, then matter, with all its bristliness, seediness, softness etc., must also be contained in the divine essence. In other words, as Patterson argues, the logical conclusion of Aquinas' argument that a community of nature exists between divine ground and createde ffect is that God must be, in some sense, material.[17] Or, taken from the other direction, given the logic of the "community of nature" doctrine, if God is absolutely other than matter, how is he its source and cause?

Secondly, Aquinas' resolution assumes that bare undifferentiated being can imply a multitude of modes of being, so that to know being in its simplicity is to know it in its multiplicity. Aquinas' argument here is based not upon logic or analogy but upon the sheer transcendent mystery of the divine mode of knowing. Difficulties arise as soon as we ask whether there are any grounds of any sort for holding that plurality can be intuited (God's mode of knowing) form bare identity (God's mode of being). What is at issue here is whether it is a possibility for thought to hold that what is not distinct in fact (the divine essence) can be the source of knowledge of what is distinct in fact (the plurality of the creation). For example, how would the knowledge of a wholly undifferentiated insect imply the particularities of the thousands of forms of insect life down to their finest variation. The argument that this kind of reasoning is not at all applicable to our thought on God is based wholly on the viability of the notion that God is pure act, without shadow of change or potentiality of being. But it is precisely the viability of this traditional concept of God that has come under question in case after case. Surely sufficient problems have been raised regarding the concept of God as pure being to forbid the rejection of a line of reasoning sheerly on the basis that God is witthout potentiality.

In sum, I would like to argue that in the area of the divine knowledge Aquinas' thought cannot intelligibly sustain itself when it seeks to work out the problem of the one and the many, the simple

---

[17] Patterson, *The Concept of God in the Philosophy of Aquinas*, p. 128.

and the complex. If this is granted, then we are faced with an either-
or situation. Either the divine knowledge is structurally complex or
the divine knowledge excludes any definite plurality. Aquinas, for
obvious theological reasons, holds that God knows distinctions.
The discussion, then, can move past the issue of the structural complexity of God's knowledge, and onto the more basic issue of whether
that complexity is absolutely and ultimately underived complexity
or whether it is, at the least, in part relatively derived complexity.
This issue is, I would argue, the trinitarian issue, and it will be pi-
cked up in the discussion of that doctrine. For the present, I want
to turn to the doctrine of the *analogia entis* and argue that the doctrine of simplicity undermines this mode of knowing God.

The ground of man's knowledge of an infinite God is the corollary to the ground of God's knowledge of finite things; namely,
as God contains all modes of being, so all modes of being partially participate, some more, some less, in the infinite totality of being.[18]
On this basis, then, that all modes of being are derived from God,
Aquinas formulates the analogy of proportionality. The crux of this
doctrine is that there must be a similarity of proportions between
a finite being and his attributes and the divine being and his attributes.[19] Thus, the analogy of proportionality rests upon (1) the
possibility of establishing a ratio between the two orders of being
(infinite, eternal being and finite, temporal being) and (2) the assumption of a differentiation in the infinite analogous to (or similar
to) the relation of subject-predicate in the finite. The critical problem
arises from the fact that Aquinas understands infinity in terms of
simplicity. God's infinity, for Aquinas, does not merely mean that
he is unlimited in power, goodness, etc., but beyond that it means
God is unlimited because he transcends all limitation, relation and
division.[20] In other words, God's infinity refers to the indivisable
mode of his being. God, then, has no attributes, for what are attributes in man are eminently possessed by God, and the content of
this term "eminence" is that what are called attributes in man are
fused into identity in the divine being. Thus, there can be, ontologically speaking, no talk of God standing in relation to his attributes, for God in his being is beyond attributes and therefore beyond

---

[18] Summa Ia, 13.7; De Pot. 3.3.
[19] Summa Ia, 13.5.
[20] C. G. I, 43.1, 3 : Summa Ia. 7-1.

internal relations. In sum, the multiple perfections of the creatures, which constitute in man the basis for speaking of a relation between a subject and his attributes, simply do not exist in God. In deity, according to Aquinas, the diversity of qualities and attributes achieve their perfection precisely because they lose their distinction from each other and from the being to which they belong.

Aquinas' aim in his language about God is twofold. On the one hand, it is to insist upon the incommensurability of the finite to the infinite. Thus, he holds that "we cannot grasp what God is, but only what He is not and how other things are related to Him."[21] In this vein, Aquinas stresses the inconceivable unity of God, reminding us that all diversity of concepts regarding deity does not touch the divine essence but is to be referred to the weakness of the human intellect.[22] On the other hand, in order to metaphysically legitimize our language about God, Aquinas maintains the ontological validity of analogous predication. These two aims simply will not stand together. The idea of proportions presupposes complex and finite beings, and therefore the method of analogy is fit for relations only between limited and "composed" entities. In other words, the method of analogy requires that there be distinctions in God in fact, and not simply in concept. For if there are no parts in God which could be in an analogical relation to the predicates in finite being, then, metaphysically speaking, the analogy of proportionality is valueless.[23]

Again, we arrive at an either-or situation. Either God is simple and we can say nothing further metaphysically about him, or the method of analogy is ontologically legitimate so that there is, at least in principle, the possibility for valid knowledge about God. The point is we cannot have it both ways. My own view is that is we make seriously Aquinas' insistence on a community of nature between cause and effect, and therefore between creator and creature, we can think our way through to a legitimate metaphysical ground for analogous predication. But if we do so, then we must give up Aquinas' distinction between diversity in concept and simplicity in fact. Thus, the difficulties that Aquinas' thought creates for the method of

---

[21] Summa Ia, 30.4.

[22] C. G. Ia, 30.2-4 : Summa Ia, 1.12.

[23] My critique of the doctrine of analogy here owes much to Martin Foss, *The Idea of Perfection*, (Princeton : Princeton University Press, 1946), pp. 39 ff., and to Patterson, *The Concept of God in the Philosophy of Aquinas*, pp. 244 ff.

analogy can be resolved by moving towards the notion of ontological complexity. Aquinas, of course, refused to make this move.

There is, then, a tension in Aquinas' thought. On the one hand, his doctrine of analogy implies a movement in his thought toward the idea of God's ontological complexity; on the other hand, his doctrine of simplicity denies the legitimacy of the analogical method by asserting the absolute oneness of God. Aquinas was certainly aware of this tension but he never gave up the primacy of the notion of devine simplicity. The reason for this is that Aquinas understands the notion of simplicity as inherently connected with the perfection of God. It is necessary to closely analyse this connection closely and draw out its implications.

Aquinas maintains that "a thing is perfect in proportion to its state of actuality because we call that perfect which lacks nothing of the mode of its perfection."[24] Perfection, then, is a function of the actualization of the potentialities of being. Given this understanding of perfection, Aquinas sees the task of guarding God's perfection as consisting in the denial of all language which suggests the presence of unactualized potentiality in God. It is for this reason that he regards God not only as the eternal ground and power of all being but as the full actualization of all being from eternity. Therefore, God's knowledge, power, goodness, will, etc., must be complete, for a lack of completion in any aspect of the divine being would constitute a lack in perfection. Simillary, God's existence must be identical with his essence, he must be his predicates rather than merely possess them, for if any distinction were allowed here the full actualization of the divine being would be questioned, For the same reason God must be *a se*, totally self-sufficent, the fullness of his concrete being must come absolutely from himself, his knowledge must be of himself, his own being must constitute his only end, his will must be his own good, etc.; in sum, his act must be his own being.

What is significant here is that it is Aquinas' understanding of perfection which leads to the notion of the "purity" of God's act of being, and it is precisely the absolute quality of this "purity" of act which makes God absolutely simple. Thus, Aquinas' notion of perfection becomes in fact the notion of oneness, or more accurately, the notion of identity. God's power is not related to his

---

[24] Summa I 4.1.

goodness, it is identical with goodness; his will is not related to his aim, it is identical with his aim; his act is not related to his being, it is identical with his being. This ontology of identity is the ground of the denial of both real relations within deity and real, internal relations between God and the world.[25] Thus, in Aquinas' thought on God, the principle of relation becomes the coincidence of distinctions, so that in fact relation comes to mean identity. In the end, then, the idea of divine perfection depends upon the contradiction of the principle of relation; that is, identity is a relation which does not relate anything. Aquinas may make use of the language of relation in his concept of God, but in every case the two sides of the relation coincide : for example, God knows the world (which implies a real relation of God to the world), by knowing himself (which denies a real relation to the world).

What emerges from this discussion is the realization that Aquinas' understanding of perfection as identity lies at the root of his denial of relations and distinctions.[26] As I have argued throughout, it is this denial of relations and distinctions which threatens the coherence of the whole fabric of Aquinas' concept of God. That Thomas was aware of this threat is reflected in his movement from the *via negativa*[27] to the *via analogia*. That is, Thomas saw that to move beyond saying what God is not like, and therefore leaving to sheer incomprehensibility what God is like, he had to shift the basis of his method from how God is not ontologically related to the world to how he is related.

Nevertheless, the problem remains, as I noted earlier, that the *via analogia* can validly be used only where there are distinctions and relations in deity. "The frenzy of identity"[28] which lies behind the ideas of simplicity, oneness, perfection, essence equals existence, etc., obviously provides no ontological basis for the *via analogia* and ultimately, undermines its cogency within the framework of Aquinas' thought. Thus the *via analogia* stands out in Aquinas' system as a method looking for its proper ontology; namely, an ontology of divine complexity. Now that kind of ontology, on the

---

[25] Though God is, of course, "externally" related to the world - cf. Summa Ia, 13.7; C. G. II, 12.

[26] The historical roots of Aquinas' thought here is a separate issue : cf. the discussion of the idea of perfection in Aristotle in Foss, *op. cit.*, pp. 18-22.

[27] Summa Ia, 3. preface.

[28] A peculiarly forceful phrase of Foss', *The Idea of Perfection*, p. 22.

surface at least, seems to be suggested by trinitarian thinking about God, with pluralism, distinctions, and relations. The situation is that Thomas, in confronting the doctrine of the trinity, saw his task as reconciling trinitarian relationalism with the logic of identity. My argument is that the tension generated by this attempted reconciliation points the way through to a Christian doctrine of divine relativity.

CHAPTER VII

TRINITARIAN THEOLOGY

Two texts bring out the situation that faced Aquines as he sought to place the doctrine of the trinity within the framework of his absolute notion of God :

Moreover, a thing has being in the manner it possesses unity. Hence each thing struggles as much as it can against any division of itself, lest thereby it tend to non-being. But the divine nature has being most powerfully. There is therefore, in it the greatest unity, and hence no plurality is in any way distinguished within it.[1]

There are several real relations in God; and hence it follows that there are also several realities subsistent in the divine nature; which means that there are several persons in God.[2]

The notion of "several realities subsistent in the divine nature" is for Aquinas a revealed notion given in scripture.[3] His task, as he understands it, lies in reconciling the revelation of distinctions with the rational concept of absolute unity.

Aquinas makes a tentative stab at this problem by turning to his familiar distinction of logical and real relations. Thus, he maintains that "relation as referred to the essence does not differ there from in reality, but only in our way of thinking."[4] That is, the distinction between the absolute essence and several realities in deity do not point to ontological distinctions but to logical or conceptual ones. Thomas, however, cannot adopt unqualifiedly this kind of solution to the trinitarian distinctions, for it could only lead to the "persons" in God losing their reality in favor of the divine essence.

---

[1] C. G. I, 42.18.
[2] Summa Ia, 30.1.
[3] Summa Ia, 32.1.
[4] Summa Ia, 39.1.

Instead, he takes the more subtle (paradoxical) position that the distinctions in deity are conceptual only in relation to the absoluteness of the divine essence, while in reference to that which is relative in God – namely, the several realities of Father, Son, and Spirit – they point to real distinctions.[5] In other words, Thomas assumes that he can make stand the argument that a "plurality of relations... do not import composition in that of which they are predicated."[6]

Now Thomas knows well enough that he lacks the language that would enable him to speak at once of the absolute simplicity of God and the plurality of relations within him.[7] The crucial issue, however, in the doctrine of the Trinity, is not that of the inadequacy of language or, for that matter, of logic. Aquinas can attribute difficulties in language and in logic to the mystery of God, holding that what constitutes incoherence according to the logic of finite being is not necessarily incoherent according to the logic of infinite being.[8]

The reason why logic and language have always been considered the main problem of trinitarian thought is that it has been traditionally assumed that the doctrine of the trinity must be reconciled with the doctrine of simplicity. A different perspective is gained if the problem raised by trinitarian thought is understood as the questioning of the doctrine of simplicity. The tradition which Aquinas inherited, and which he maintained, never really asked itself whether the metaphysical implications of trinitarian thinking are really at one with the metaphysical implications of "simplitarian" thinking. It simply assumed their oneness and sought to reconcile the problems of logic as best it could. But what if the problem lies not with logic but with the ontology of the absolute that underlies the notion of divine simplicity? In that case the questions put to Aquinas' trinitarian thought should concern the character of its metaphysical

[5] Summa Ia, 28.3, 39.1.

[6] Summa Ia, 30.1.

[7] See Summa Ia, 29.4 where Thomas discusses his acceptance of the inherited term "person" to signify "relation as subsisting in the divine nature", despite his awareness that, in its ordinary usage, person signifies an individual thing that exists in itself and not in another.

[8] This is, of course, the ultimate rationale for God as an exception to all metaphysical principles. The problem in making God an ontological exception is that, in principle, it breaks down rational and empirical guidelines for genuine knowledge of God.

implications. This will shift the trinitarian discussion towards the issue of the ontological compatibility of trinitarian theology and "simplitarian" thought.

Aquinas begins his discussion of the Trinity (in question 27) by holding that divine persons are distinguished by relations of origins alone; that is, the persons of the Trinity are constituted strictly by the internal relations within the one divine essence. The first term of these relations is the Father. The reason for this is that the Father is the principle of the whole deity, where "principle" is interpreted as signifying the first term of a thing.[9] The language of paternity, can be used to distinguish the person of the Father from the persons of the Son and Holy Spirit. Conversely, the second and third persons are distinguished in relation from the Father in that they take their origin from (i.e., proceed from) the Father, and they are distinguished in relation from each other in that the third person proceeds from the other two.[10]

Aquinas seeks to persuade us of the consonance of the notion of a plurality of relations within a simple being by drawning upon a psychological analysis of the divine self. The analysis goes this way : since God is pure intelligibility, in thinking of himself, God begets God. That is, God the Father's act of understanding, which issues in his Word or Logos-Son is identical with his very being. Now for God to understand, according to the logic of identity, is to be, and simillary so with his loving. That is, loving also issues in being, for God as loved by himself signifies something substantial to his essence, as opposed to something accidental to it.[11]

Thus, Aquinas suggests that the serious problems of logic in the doctrine of the Trinity can be minimized in importance by thinking of God's being as analogous to the human psyche unfolding itself in three directions. Let us examine the analogy. First, there is the thinking self, or divine intellect to use Aquinas' terminology, which duplicates itself in its consciousness of itself. The thinking self is analogous to the begetting Father, the consciousness or image of the self is analogous to the begotten Logos-Son. The Son, as the absolute or exhaustive word or image generated by the operation of the divine intellect, is one with the divine essence. Thus, the Father is identical with the divine essence, the Son is identical with the

[9] Summa Ia. 33.1.
[10] Summa Ia. 32.3.
[11] Summa Ia, 27.3.

divine essence, and therefore, though they are distinguished in relation by differentiation of origin, they are one in essence.

Out of the relation that exists between Father and Son, there arises a second process, analogous to the self willing to love itself, and this is the love that binds the intellect to the image which it conceived. This process, then which for want of a better word, Aquinas calls the spiration (from *spiratio*, breathing) of the Holy Spirit, arises out of the operation of the divine will. Since God's will is one with the divine essence, given the logic of identity, the Spirit, in essence, is identical with the divine essence, and is therefore con-substantial with and co-equal to the Father and Son. In sum, the three distinct realities of the Trinity are symbolized by the language of God's eternal objectification of himself in his image and the eternal unity of himself in the love that he bears for himself.

Aquinas, then, in the opening articles of the trinitarian discussion, tends to think of the persons of the Trinity as strictly internal processes which exist in deity "only according to an action which does not tend to anything external, but remains in the agent itself."[12] There is good reason for Aquinas' inclination towards the psychological analogy. First of all, the analogy is self-contained and reciprocal in its relations (God must both know and love himself). More important, a psychological analogy may lend itself to the logic of identity, and therefore is ontologically amenable to the notion of divine simplicity of being. Its shortcoming is that lacks full adequacy to the trinitariun situation. The reason for this is that according to trinitarian doctrine the termini of the psychological analogy, namely self-knowledge and self-love, must symbolize not simply the internal operations of a distinct self but must symbolize hypostases; that is, they must include the dimension of a distinct, individual reality. It is precisely where Aquinas wrestles with the issue of the hypostatic reality of the several persons that the issue of consonance with the idea of simplicity gets sharply raised. Let us turn to this discussion.

As noted above, what distinguished the Father from the other persons, is the quality of Paternity; namely, the Father is the ultimate (unbegotten) reality, and the other divine realities proceed from him. This notion of paternity in its unqualified form tends to suggest that the Father is a distinct reality in contradistinction to Son and

---

[12] Summa Ia, 27.3.

Spirit. In order to maintain the doctrine that no essential distinctions exist within deity, Aquinas holds that there is a sense in which "unbegotten" can be understood as strictly a relative term, as opposed to a substantial one. His argument is that the meaning of "unbegotten" is relative to its opposing term. Thus, where "unbegotten" is terminologically opposed to "created," it signifies the substantial distinction between uncreated and created entities. On the other hand, where "unbegotten" is opposed not to what is created but but to what is begotten, then it implies relation and can be properly used to signify the hypostatic relation whithin deity. There are semantic weaknesses in this argument : "begotten" is merely defined, by fiat, as not having an ontological significance similar to "created." This, unfortunately, does not advance the discussion since it is not at all clear why the power to beget, unlike the power to create, does not involve a distinction in essence. More significant, Aquinas himself is unable to consistently maintain unbegottenness as sheerly an immanent relational term that is inapplicable to any divine external action.

We begin then, with Aquinas' position that the divine persons are distinguished by relations of origin alone so that "procession exists in God only according to an action which does not tend to anything external, but remains in the agent itself."[13] Aquinas' intention here is to deny any correlation between the external actions of deity and the trinitarian distinctions of origin. The reason for this is that given his understanding of the nature of a thing is its principle of operation, each person would differ in nature if his external actions were specifically grounded in any given distinction of relation. Aquinas protects trinitarianism from tri-theism (three divine natures) by asserting the oneness of external operations, the essential identity of the three persons with the divine nature[14] and the equality of the persons[15]. Thus Aquinas reaffirms the traditional notion of mutual indwelling or perichoresis, the view that neither the nature of the persons, nor their actions, can be divided or separately conceived but mutually exist in one another.[16] Hence,

[13] Summa Ia. 27.3.

[14] Summa Ia. 42.3.

[15] In question forty-two of the Summa, Aquinas sets forth five grounds for the equality of Father, Son and Spirit : identity of essence, coeternity of person, equality of perfection, mutual indwelling, equality of power.

[16] See above, Chapter I, Section V, for a full discussion of perichoresis.

via the logic of identity, the concept of simplicity retains its primacy in informing the doctrine of God. Here, as elsewhere, the logic
of identity is used to smother distinctions. What is ironical, as sub-
sequent discussion will show, is that its use in trinitarian theology
will undermine the very idea of divine absoluteness which evoked
it in the first place.

Both the doctrine of perichoresis and the logic of ontological
identity break down for Aquinas precisely where they break down
for Augustine, namely in the doctrine of mission, the sending of
the Son by the Father. What happens is that "perichoresis" runs
into some Biblical and philosophical complications. Biblically,
it runs into the mission texts : e.g. "when the fullness of time was
come, God sent his son;[17] philosophically, it runs into the notion
of the absolute aseity of God – the denial of relativity in the divine
being. The key passages are the following :

as the Father is not from another, in no way is it fitting for Him to be
sent, but this can only belong to the son and to the Holy Ghost to whom
it belongs to be from another[18]

The thought is elaborated :

as implying the authority of the giver as regards what is given, to be given
only applies in God to the person who is from another; and the same
as regards being sent.[19]

What is clear from these statements is that contrary to his inten-
tions (in the doctrine of perichoresis) Thomas strictly correlates
(in the doctrine of missions) the actions of the deity with the trinitarian relations of origin. The Father cannot be sent because
he is unbegotten; on the other hand, he has the authority to send
because he is the begetter. Similary the Son can be sent, but
only by the Father, and he has the authority to send the Holy
Spirit, who proceeds from the Father and the Son. In the case of
the Holy Spirit, there is no authority whatsoever to send, but only
to be sent. In other words, the doctrine of temporal missions, in
establishing of authority and external actions, presupposes ontological distinctions whithin deity (it is not the Father's nature to
be sent, etc.,). The obvious point of the discussion here is that the

[17] Gal. 4.4.
[18] Summa Ia, 43.4.
[19] Summa Ia, 43.4.

doctrine of perichoresis, with its ideas of mutuality, immanence, and joint action, has been set aside (and with it, the careful arguments for the equality of the persons). For example, if followed consistently, the doctrine of perichoresis would have had the whole deity incarnate, and the Son would have been said to be sent only in the sense of "appropriation."[20]

I discussed earlier[21] the main reasons why orthodox trinitarian thought does not avail itself of the doctrines of perichoresis and appropriations in the area of temporal missions. Basically, it has to do with refusal to surrender the Hellenic notion that the godness of God consists in his non-relativity. Perichoresis would involve the whole deity in relations to the world; the doctrine of temporal missions denies this by continuing to think of the Father as symbolic of that godness of God which is the "monadic" independence of perfection. In other words, the doctrine of missions is really a relic of the early logos heritage which subordinated the Son and Spirit to the absoluteness of the Father.

The problem regarding the doctrine of temporal missions is not simply its incoherency alongside the doctrine of perichoresis, but its functioning as a roadblock to a line of relational thinking that trinitarianism had begun to move along. The doctrines of perichoresis and appropriations arise out of the necessity to maintain a monotheistic theology within an incarnational faith. These doctrines are part of the very technical trinitariun thinking of the early church, but they can be thought of more significantly as marking the beginning of an incarnational ontology; that is, an ontology which takes account of the incarnational dimension of religious faith. What I want to argue is that Aquinas' reaffirmation of the Patristic doctrine of missions simply serves to continue forestalling the development of a (Trinitarian) relational ontology in in order to maintain the Hellenic ontology of the absolute. If this argument is essentially correct, then it should be capable of demonstration that Thomas' exposition of the Trinity, despite his "mission" thought, implicitly moves away from the ontology of the absolute. I want to try to make that case.

---

[20] The doctrine of "appropriation" is treated in the Summa Ia, 39; see above, Chapter I, section vi, for the discussion of "appropriation" in the thought of St. Augustine.

[21] See above Chapter I, section vi.

In the context of the argument that "Word" is the most (metaphysically) appropriate name for the second person of the Trinity,[22] Aquinas reminds us that for each thing that we understand, we denote different words. "Word," then, as a categoreal term, serves to represent everything that is actually understood by the mind. From this, he argues :

because God by his one act understands himself and all things, His one only Word is expressive not only of the Father, but of all creatures... because in the Word is implied the operative idea of what God makes.[23]

Somewhat earlier in the *Summa*, Aquinas had expressed this thought even more emphatically :

the Father, by understanding Himself, the Son, and the Holy Ghost, and all other things contained within his knowledge, conceives the Word, and thus the entire Trinity and every created being are uttered in the Word.[24]

In these passages, two dimensions of the divine knowledge are being distinguished : the first embraces the divine self-comprehension, the second the divine comprehension of the created order. The significant point is that, according to these passages, these two kinds of knowledge constitute one act of cognition, that is, both of them belong to the knowledge of God as God. It is true that in *De veritate*, Aquinas qualifies his thought by distinguishing between the Word as principally referring to the Father "and only consequently, and, as it were, by accident" referring to the creatures.[25] This distinction, however, is strictly an abstract conceptual one. If the Father, in uttering Himself (i.e., in the eternal begetting of the Son), also utters the world, then the distinctions of "principally" and "accidentally" are abstractions from the concrete relationalism of divine and creaturely being. For if knowledge of the created order is an eternal dimension of the divine knowledge, then God and the world, according to trinitarian thinking, are essentially or ontologically mutual implicates.[26] If this interpretation is

---

[22] Summa Ia, 34.3.

[23] Summa Ia, 34.3.

[24] Summa Ia, 34.1. ad 3; cf. De Ver. 4.4.

[25] De Ver. 4.4.

[26] Cf. J. Pohle and A. Preuss, *The Divine Trinity*, (St. Louis, Mo., B. Herder Book Co., 1930), pp. 213-214 for support of this interpretation : (Knowledge of self and world are) "essential and absolutely necessary to the very being of the Godhead".

correct, then the God implied by Trinitarian thinking is clearly
at variance with the absolute notion of God that Aquinas had earlier set forth.

A similar kind of interpretation emerges from Aquinas' discussion
of the term Gift as the proper name of the third person. Aquinas
argues (in question 37) that the Holy Spirit is the love proceeding
to the Son necessarily and the creatures concomitantly and ac-
cidently.[27] Given this, he holds that "love has the nature of a first
gift, in strength whereof all free gifts are given."[28] Aquinas then
deals with the objection that to call a divine preson "gift from eternity" is to involve deity in a necessary relation to the world (i.e.,
it implies the necessity of an other" to receive the gift). His answer
to this objection is that, in the divine case, "Gift is not called from
being actually given, but from its aptitude to be given... Hence,
the divine person is called Gift from eternity although He is given
in time."[29] It is difficult, however, to see how this answer would
satisfy Thomas' objectors. For what they are objecting to is precisely the fact that the logic of God's eternal and absolute mode
being forbids the language of "aptitude." The reason for this is
that according to the tradition what God gives, He gives eternally,
in a once-for-all given, so that there can be no distinction in God
between actuality and aptitude. On the other hand, to affirm such
a distinction implies a potential aspect of being.

Now what Aquinas is arguing for, against his orthodox and more
consistent objectors, is the notion that the Holy Spirit does not
express merely God's eternal love for Himself, but that concomitantly, it eternally expresses God's love for the created universe.
Clearly Aquinas is seeking in trinitarian thought the ontological
ground for the Biblical affirmation "God so loved the world."
The language of "gift" serves to protect this affirmation, but "gift"
as his critics fear suggests a social ontology. In other words, we
have arrived at another point where trinitarian thought and language imply a concept of being at variance with the absolute being
worked out in the theology of divine perfections. What then is the
ontology of God that is implied by trinitarian thinking?

Aquinas holds that God's act of understanding, which is the

---

[27] This is the Pohle-Preuss formulation of the distinction; cf. *ibid.*, p. 218.
[28] Summa Ia, 38.2.
[29] Summa Ia, 38.1.

begetting of the Word, and his act of love, which is the procession of the Holy Spirit, are identical with the divine essence. This dictum protects his trinitarian thought from moving into either Tritheism or modalism. That is, God the Father does not generate new gods or different episodes of the same God. Rather, what the Father begets and spirates is the divine nature, so that the three persons are identical in nature. Thus when trinitarian doctrine holds that the Logos represents[30] the divine comprehension of self and world, and the Holy Spirit represents the divine self-love and world love, it is implying that the godness of God (i.e., his nature and existence) pre-supposes a self-world relation. In this way trinitarian theology moves away implicitly from the notion that God can have the fullness of His being apart from the being of the world.

The sum of my argument is this : the logic of trinitarian thought points to a relational or social notion of divine being. It is the Father that begets, but the Father does not beget the Son out of nothing, but out of the divine nature [31]. Given that the nature of a thing for Aquinas is the principle of its action, we can arrive at the kind of being that is expressed by the trinitarian thought by looking at the outcome of begetting (and spirating). Now the language used here concerns both the self and the world, namely, self-understanding and world undrstanding, self-love and world-love. The being implied by this language is surely one whose self-identity transcends world identity (patheism is excluded), but the meaning of this language is missed if it is not also clear that the being implied here is one whose self-identity is, in part, informed by the world's identity. Thus, the argument here coincides with my earlier argument that God's knowledge and love of a world requires that we posit a reciprocal relation between the being of the world and divine being.

This social understanding of God's being qualifies the orthodox notion of God as an absolute and atomic being.[32] Absoluteness

---

[30] The use of the form "re-present" is deliberate; the Father is not "wise" by the Son, nor "love" by the Holy Spirit, but he is "wise" and "love" by the divine essence which is identical in the three persons; cf. Summa Ia, 37.2, 39.7.

[31] Summa Ia, 41.5.

[32] The view presented here should not be confused with Hodgson's "social analogy of the Trinity". Hodgson retains the absolute notion of God, and interprets the Doctrine of the Trinity as a way of protecting the notion of divine personality in the face of a doctrine of absoluteness. (Cf. Leonard Hodgson,

here is understood as an abstraction so that such notions as pure being or pure act can be seen as conceptions arising out of a process of abstracting from the actuality of concrete and interrelated activity. Thus, it is not in the theology of the divine perfections, but in Trinitarian theology that we find the expression of the "whole" God. In Trinitarian theology we find the relational concepts of Word and Spirit and not the concepts of absolute mind and absolute will. The word of God, as the expression of the supreme power of the divine intellect to understand all created things, symbolizes a supremely related mind. The Holy Spirit, as the expression of the love of God for every creature, symbolizes a supremely related will.

The notion of a supremely related being requires a redefination of the idea of perfection. Perfection, here, cannot mean an absence of potentiality or possibilities, but a maximization of the potential power of mind and act in order to allow for full envisionment of and adequate response to every activity thrown up by the world. In *The Logic of Perfection*, Hartshorne has argued that "unactualized possibilities increase rather than decrease with the rank of being.[33] This kind of insight suggests that the perfection of God lies in the quality of the relative response rather than in the priority of the (absolute) act. This last point sets the task for the final chapter.

The Doctrine of the Trinity, (New York : Scribner's, 1944), p. 190, and Summa Ia, 28.3 ad 4 for Aquinas' rejection of the social analogy as he found it in Richard of St. Victor). On the other hand, Cyril Richardson sees clearly that the doctrine of the Trinity arose out of the struggle of the Platonically informed fathers wrestling with a way to speak at once of God's absolute independence from the world and his involvement in it. The difficulty in Professor Richardson's thought arises out of its ontological instability. Richardson's argument that there is no way of relating God's absoluteness with his relativity results in an inner contradiction of being in the very ground of being.

[33] Hartshorne, *The Logic of Perfection*, p. 37.

CHAPTER VIII

REDEMPTION AND PROCESS THEISM

The tensions engendered by the traditional use of the absolute categories find their corollary in the abandonment of these categories in Trinitarian theology. This statement represents the critical side of this study. The constructive side centers around the proposition that the logical and moral difficulties thrown up by orthodoxy can be met by the social view of deity suggested by Trinitarian theology and worked out in the metaphysics of Whitehead. Such a view admitting temporality, relativity and process into the Such a view entails admitting temporality, relativity and process into the divine life.

The temporality of God refers to the temporal coincidence between the events of the world and God's experience of them. The relativity of God signifies the mutual requiring of each other by God and the world. Process, in deity, affirms the many occasions of the world becoming one in the divine life and increasing the content of that life by one.

The immediate problem in such a view stems from the recognition that what is gained in logic is lost in terms of God's final transcendence. There are three broad objections. The first stems from the belief that the admission of temporality into divine being qualifies the divine wisdom. The argument is that God's inability to know the future in its detail precludes the perfection of divine activity; God must act in accordance with an estimate of the world's response, and that estimate may turn out wrong. In a similar way, relativity qualifies the divine power. Here the problem is that only the unlimited power of absolute being can assure the realization of God's final purposes. The objection is that an idea of God that does not provide this guarantee is religiously inadequate. Finally, it is argued that the admission of process into deity qualifies the divine majesty. A god that is part of the furniture of the universe is religiously unsatisfying – provoking neither awe nor worship.

These objections voice genuine religious concerns. Religion is first and foremost a phenomenon, and only derivately a doctrine. This means that these concerns cannot be ignored; they must be either safeguarded or critically re-evaluated. Cyril Richardson's radical interpretation of the Trinity is, in fact, a conservative safeguarding of traditional religious concerns rather than a radical rethinking of those concerns. The genius of Richardson's thought lies in its attempt to meet, through the dogma of the Trinity, the logical and moral objections to the concept of absolute being without losing the "religious requisite" of the absolute categories. What he does is to slough off neither the relative Biblical categories nor the absolute Hellenic categories; he sees both as presupposed by our faith in a redeemer God and therefore he affirms both as essential of divine being. Thus, the godness of God lies not in his absolutenes but in his (paradoxically) being absolute in all respects and yet also relative.

The strength of Richardson's argument hangs upon two interrelated assumptions : that man's redemptive faith loses its genuine ground where the divine absoluteness is compromised; and that religious theism has reached the limits of language and logic and therefore must rest with a logically incoherent concept of deity. The question before us, then, is whether a process theology which qualifies the divine power, wisdom, etc. can account for a redemptive faith. Richardson himself rejects the Whiteheadian wiew on the grounds that its failure to apply all the absolute qualities uncompromisingly threatens the ultimate relevancy of God's fixity of purpose. God is not really God, he argues, but "is part of a process greater than he is, and one which may eventually be victorious over him."[1]

The "process" that Richardson is referring to has been described by Whitehead as "the creative advance into novelty"[2] or, more simply creativity. Richardson might aptly remind us here that Whitehead holds that both God and the world "are in the grip of (this) ultimate metaphysical ground."[3] Thus, in some sense, a Whiteheadian view binds God to the creative process. The question is

---

[1] Cyril Richardson, "The Ontological Trinity : Father and Son", *Religion in Life*, Vol. XXVIII, p. 15.

[2] Alfred North Whitehead, *Process and Reality*, (New York : Macmillan, 1929), pp. 10-11.

[3] PR, pp. 31-32. John Cobb has collected a number of Whitehead passages

whether the sense of that binding is such that it poses a threat to the redemptive relevance of God. The answer to this question depends upon the metaphysical status of creativity. The following passage will bring us to the center of the matter :

> In all philosophic theory there is an ultimade which is actual in virtue of its accidents. It is only then capable of characterization through its accidental embodiments, and apart from these accidents is devoid of actuality. In the philosophy of organism this ultimate is termed 'creativity'; and God is its primordial, non-temporal accident.[4]

Two points are particularly important in this and will require some elaboration. First, apart from its exemplifications, creativity is devoid of actuality. Whitehead terms creativity "the universal of universals characterizing ultimate matter of fact"; with the 'many' and the 'one', it is an "ultimate notion... presupposed in all the more special categories."[5] In other words, creativity is not an entity or thing, "not an external agency with its own ulterior purposes,"[6] but a general activity exhibited by all entities, things and agents. Whatever is, emerges from a past, has an inherent referance to its environment and looks towards a future which in some measure must take account of its present activity. There is no way of having one's being apart from exemplifying this activity, and, in this sense, creativity is transcendent to each particular actuality; in this sense, whatever is, is "in the grip" of creativity. On the other hand, there is no creative process apart from the activity of the actual entities-individual actualities alone constitute the "final realities."[7] This means that the transcendence of creativity is analogous to the transcendence of the generalization to the embodied instance; it is not analogous to the transcendence of one mode of being in relation to another.[8]

---

which suggest the subordination of God to creativity. See *A Christian Natural Theology*, (Philadelphia : Westminster, 1965), pp. 167-8, 204.

[4] PR, p. 339.
[5] PR, pp. 31-32.
[6] PR, p. 339.
[7] PR, p. 32.
[8] "There are not two actual entities, the creativity and the creature. There is only one entity which is the self-creating creature". *Religion in the Making*, (New York : Macmillan, 1926), p. 102.

There is another sense in which actual entities constitute the "final realities." and its discussion will clarify the second point regarding the metaphysical status of the creative process. For Whitehead, the reason for things is not to be found in forms, structures, principles or ideas as such. Precisely where Whitehead is anti-Platonic is in his dictum that "actual entities are the reasons; so that to search for a reason is to search for one or more actual entities."[9] Creativity is an ultimate notion and not an actual entity, which means that it functions as neither an efficient nor final cause. The search for the reason for the embodiment of the creative process must be the search for that actual entity which Whitehead calls a primordail, non-temporal accident. Two points here : God is, first of all, a non-temporal accident, which is to say that the fact of his being is an ultimate irrationality – there is no explanation for it, no getting behind his existence, God is simply an everlasting given. Secondly, God is primordial or originative; he is ontologically presupposed by the world.

Whitehead, then, understands God as metaphysically required by the very fact of the ongoingness of the world. Here his thought parallels Aquinas', and yet there is a crucial divergence. Aquinas conceives God as providing the power to be required by all finite actualities for their existence. In other words the power to act, for Aquinas, finds its ultimate ground in the divine being.[10] For Whitehead, the general activity of creativity characterizes all being, the being of God and the being of the merest puff of existence. Monism then is excluded; the power to be is pluralistic. This means that a phrase such as the "power to be" refers not to an actual existent but to a characteristic of being exemplified by both God and the world. Herein lies the decisive point where Whitehead qualifies the traditional concept of God. God, for Whitehead, is not the ground of being, he is the ground of definiteness. This point requires some expansion.

In Chapter XI of *Science and the Modern World*, the concept of God was introduced into Whitehead's philosophy via the argument that to be does not simply mean to become, but to become

[9] PR, p. 37. This basic category of explanation is termed the ontological principle.

[10] The theological counterpart of this metaphysical notion is the doctrine of creatio ex nihilo which secures God's absolute supremacy by conceiving the world as absolutely dependent upon deity for its creation.

something definite. This being the case, Whitehead argues that the structured nature of things presupposes a ground of definiteness; what he called in SMW, a principle of limitation or concretion. In other words, if there is to be anything at all, there must be a limiting principle which is the order given to or drawn upon by any subject moving to a particular, definite outcome.

In *Process and reality*, Whitehead clarifies and develops the functions of the primordial character of God within the framework of a metaphysical scheme and opens up his concept of God to include a "consequent" or concrete pole of divine being.[11]

As primordial, God is the complete conceptualization of all possibilities of definiteness, presenting those relavent to his creatures as they are drawn towards some definite actualization. In making a novel possibility theoretically available to an original entity in the temporal world, and in evoking appetition for that possibility, God conditions though not determines, the ongoing activity of the world. The reason for this limitation of divine power is that the initial aim for realization that God provides for each creature is itself limited in two ways.

First, the maximum good for any particular occasion is always the maximum good compatible with the situation. "The initial stage of its aim, "Whitehead writes, "is an endowment which the subject inherits from the inevitable ordening of things, conceptually realized in the nature of God... The initial aim is the best for that impasse."[12] Thus, the past occasions of the world, specifically as they are physically experienced by the consequent nature ol God, condition the primordial, ordering activity of God. The upshot of this is that "God and the (past) actual world jointly constitute the character of the creativity for the initial phase of the novel (entity)."[13]

Secondly, in evoking form and definiteness out of the world, God elicits the self-creation of actualities. Thus, the initial aim that God provides for an original entity is limited by that entity's modification of it; "whatever is determinable is determined, but there is always a remainder for the decision of the subject."[14] This deci-

---

[11] Whitehead makes it clear that this distinction in the divine being is "a distinction of reason"; the primordial nature of God, considered apart from the consequent nature, is "God in the abstraction of a primordial actuality". PR 521-522.

[12] PR, p. 373.

[13] PR, p. 374.

sion, in fact, is the reaction of the whole to the determining sum of its parts.[15] The aspect of freedom or self-creation in the temporal world, then, is grounded in the organic response of the creature acting as the final determinant to its own internal determination.

As the principle of limitation and the provider of the initial aim, God is ever-present to the world as its creator. His creative functions are unique, universal and complete; there cannot be another God. Yet the creative course of the universe is not to be ascribed sheerly to God. God acts upon the world, but there is a (novel) reaction of the world upon God. The course of the world then need not, and obviously does not, simply conform to the purposes of God. Richardson's argument, that if God is not absolute in all aspects his fixity of purpose is threatened, is quite correct if we read *immediate* purpose. God does not wholly control finite entitites, and the range of aberration available to them precludes any fixity of response. In other words, God's immediate purposes are relative, but the point I want to argue is that his ultimate purposes are absolute and always relevant to his immediate purposes and the present course of the world.

First, the primordial or conceptual pole of deity, is not only necessary for the whole process of existence, but it is unconditioned by the direction of that process. It is presupposed by the "particularities of the actual world... while it merely presupposes the general methaphysical character of creative advance, of which it is the primordial exemplification."[16] As the pure enivisagement of possibility, it is everlasting and unchangeable eternally given with (some) world and limited by no world.[17]

Secondly, the initial aim provided for any finite actuality seeks the highest possible value relevant for each occasion. In that every existing being moves to realize some definiteness, value is constitutive of everything that is. Whitehead's thought protects God's freedom to elicit the highest value out of any particular situation by deriving "the perfection of God's subjective aim... from the

[14] PR, p. 41.

[15] PR, pp. 41-42.

[16] PR, p. 522.

[17] The price of unconditionedness in a realistic metaphysic is a deficiency in actuality. Structure is actual in the primordial nature, but there is no concrete actualization.

completeness of his primordial nature."[18] The unconditional character of the primordial nature secures the invulnerability of the primordial valuation from the particular course of things.

The initial aim provided by God takes into account not only the world's concrete activity but the world as qualified by God's concrete responses. The reference here is to the consequent nature, that side of deity which is incomplete, cumulative and derivative from the creative advance of the actual world. It is here that the world the many passes into and is transformed by the unity of God, adding "one" to the divine being. In turn, God's way of experiencing the world passes back into the world, becoming an item in the universe and qualifying world so that each temporal actuality includes it as an immediate fact of relevant experience."[19] God's purposes, then, enter into a world that already feels God's way of having the world. That is to say, the purposes of God are relative to a world incarnate with God the reality of the world already includes the reality of God. This means that the world is not to be understood as a reality over against God threatening the divine purpose. The world is not a threat to God, it is the locus of divine activity and actualized value.

The difficulty with this rejoinder is that it tends to miss an aspect of the theological criticism which has persistently dogged the Whiteheadian view. Stephen Ely, in 1942, argued that, in Whitehead's thought, the transmutation of the world's evil into a harmonious experience of value was a fact of God's life and not ours[20] and, more recently, Madden and Hare have argued that Whitehead's God is too weak to provide real assurance (to man) that evil will be overcome.[21] Ely's criticism of Whitehead – that the redemption of the world is a fact of God's life and not ours – is considerably more sophisticated than Madden and Hare's. Placed side by side, however, they suggest that the issue in Whitehead's concept of God is not whether evil can in any sense overcome God, but whether God has sufficient power *vis a vis* the evil in the world to leave man in hope rather than in despair. Put this way, the problem momentarily

[18] PR, p. 524.

[19] PR, p. 532.

[20] Stephen Ely, *The Religious Availability of Whitehead's God* (Madison, University of Wisconsin Press, 1942) esp. pp. 44-50.

[21] Edward Madden and P.H. Hare, "Evil and Unlimited Power", *The Review of Metaphysics*, Vol. XX, 2, December, 1966, pp. 278-289.

shifts from the concept of God to the meaning of redemption. As long as the meaning of redemption is tied up with a guarantee of an absolute elimination of evil, Whitehead's whole cosmology, from a religious perspective, will appear simply wrongheaded. It is clear enough that a "process" view of God does not allow us to predict the future of good and evil absolutely. But it is not so clear that a Whiteheadian perspective on divine power will not allow us to face our world of possibilities with a (realistically based) hope that overcomes the power of despiar.

The *sine qua non* of a doctrine of redemption is divine transcendence – God must be sufficiently other than the world in order to adequately exercise redemptive power over it. On the basis of the earlier discussion of Whitehead's concept of God, it is possible to summarise five ways in which a process view holds God to be transcendent in power over all temporal actualities.

First of all, God is transcendent in power by virtue of his ontological priority. God is the order upon which existence depends, so that nothing achieves definiteness without drawing upon God's primordial nature. Secondly, God's power is transcendent in its universality. The divine influence is effectively present throughout nature; no spatio-temporal limitations restrict its scope. Thirdly, God is transcendent in power as the ground of novelty. God can do for the world what it cannot do for itself; namely, elicit novel responses from present conditions. Thereby, God makes possible for the world its own creative advance. Fourthly, God is transcendent as the ground and preserver of value. God has unlimited conceptual power to supply aims relevant to all grades of being, and he is unlimited in his power to preserve and harmonize the values of the world. Finally, God is transcendent in power by virtue of the unconditioned character if his integrity. God's general aim towards the increase of value in the world and the integrity of his particular response of love towards the world are absolute.

Of course, in contrast to the orthodoxy of Aquinas, the transcendency of divine power is not absolute in all respects. Behind the traditional metaphysical affirmation of aboslute power lies the religious denial of methaphysical dualism. If God alone is the foundation of existence then nothing existent is ultimately opposed to God. The doctrine of *creatio ex nihilo* lays the cosmological ground for the eschaton – the God who created the world out of nothing will, in the end, be all in all. I do not think that we need labor the

the point that such a cosmological perspective can find tis ground in the religious experience of absolute dependence. But if this is the case, why was this traditional cosmology simply not available for Whitehead's use? The answer lies in a change in the concept of nature.

Aquinas' understanding of secondary causation was informed by the Hellenic idea that out of nothing comes nothing. Applied to the world of nature, this meant that change was intelligible only on the assumption that the actual had been pre-determined by, or already present in, the potential. Nature, then, merely becomes what it already is; fundamentally, nothing new ever happens.

This Hellenic view of nature conformed to the doctrine of *creatio ex nihilo* in that it supported the denial of any element of self-creativity in the creature. It allowed for the omnipotence of God over against the natural world, and it lent some intelligibility to the doctrine of *totum simul*. In other words, the intellectual availability of the Hellenic concept of nature permitted Aquinas to press God's transcendent power to its unlimited point. Where the movement of nature was statically conceived as the repetition of motion, nature raised no serious problems for the concepts of the absolute power, the knowledge, and the will of God.

Such a view of nature is no longer available; neither to Whitehead nor to us. The modern experience of nature is of an organic world thrusting out beyond itself, so that we look for directions as well as origins, discontinuities as well as continuity, relativity as well as individuality. This means that our understanding ol God's relation to nature must now take account of the evolutionary, social and indeterminate character of cosmic history. The modern picture of nature that we work with is one where "novelty may originate in patterns of behavior which are subsequently aided and perpetuated by mutations or variations favorable to them. The internal life of the organism is significant in producing change... (so that) higher levels of activity in organisms do influence evolutionary history."[22]

The Hellenic view of nature allowed Aquinas to conceive of divine causality in a category qualitatively apart from creaturely causality. The existence of a thing and its power to act was derived

---

[22] Ian Barbour, *Issues in Science and Religion* (Englewood Cliffs, N.J., Prentice-Hall, 1966), p. 417.

from God; nature supplied the motion from potency to actuality. This meant that God's causality did not lie amongst the causes of the world, but it underlay them as the ground or source of finite causality. Therefore, creation could be seen as an eternally transcendent and unique act of deity.

An evolutionary view, in stressing the direction and openendedness of universe, suggests that the immanent or incarnate activity of God must find a principal place in a theological doctrine of creation. Furthermore, the indeterminate character of the world, and the novelty attributable to the internal life of the creature means that the creativity of the world cannot be solely derived from divine causality. God's causality, though unique and ontologically required, nevertheless lies amongst a complexity of factors that contribute to evolutionary advance. Thus, God and the world must be seen as jointly constituting the character of the creative process. The doctrine of *creatio ex nihilo* ,as a cosmological statement, loses its intelligibility. Whitehead's understanding of the reciprocal relation of God to the world, of the one to the many, though informed by the modern concept of nature, recalls the Platonic theme that nothing is except by participation. What is different is that in our time we can more consistently take into account the full consequences of the view that being is, by its very nature, relational. There are no exceptions in Whitehead's thought to the principle that no entity has its being apart from the being of others. This is why, for Whitehead, it is more accurate to say that God's being sets the limits to his power rather than that the world sets those limits. It is not that finite powers strive against divine power but that the ontological limits in God's power allows for – and therefore makes intelligible – the real and creative power of the creature. To be is to be creative, and it is precisely because the ongoing character of things requires that God and the creature be reciprocally creative that creativity – the ultimate notion, the universal of universals, – has both God and the world in its grip.[23]

The religious criticisms directed against a process view have their roots in a particular understanding of redemption. If both God and the world are required for the creative advance of things, then,

[23] See PR, p. 528 : "God and the World are the contrasted opposites in terms of which creativity achieves its supreme task of transforming disjoined multiplicity with its diversities in opposition, into concrescent unity, with its diversities in contrast".

obviously, the absolute assurance of the realization of divine ends is precluded. The difficulty with this criticism is that it springs from a view of redemption which is tied up with the old idea of nature as a static eternally given world. The fact that we think of redemption in terms of the absence of pain, change, friction, etc., indicates that religious thought still has its feet in an outmoded concept of nature which saw completion as the state of perfection. We all know that modern science has changed our understanding of what redemption can mean, yet the criticism of Whitehead's thought, in this respect, continues to reflect a traditional understanding of redemption. Consider the following from the Madden and Hare article :

God must be very weak indeed if he is unable to move toward an aesthetic end without an enormous cost (his own and others); he is apparently so weak that he cannot guarantee his own welfare. If he is that weak, obviously he is not able, as a theistic God should be, to insure the ultimate triumph of an end of his choice, although of course he can try with absolute reliability.[24]

The three traditional assumptions about redemption are here : The realization of end (the actualization of pre-determined potential), the guarantee of that realization, the low cost of that realization (especially to God). These assumptions must be radically brought into question : the concept of redemption which must finally serve as the judge of the availability or not of Whitehead's thought for religion, must be informed by the modern not the Hellenic concept of nature.

Surely, there is a good deal of senseless pain in the world – mere wreckage – and I am not about to justify that; but equally surely, the measure of how much life does mean, to us, to God, lies precisely in the enormous cost in pain that we and God are willing to pay in order to maintain and increase the value of life. We do not have higher forms of consciousness apart from an increase in the sensitivity to pain, both our pain and that of others. The desire to be, whether that desire be conscious or not, is a quality of existence as such, and it is a blunt fact that the evolutionary advance into higher forms of existence is attained and sustained in and through an increase in the consciousness of pain. The lilies of the field neither toil nor suffer.

[24] Madden and Hare, "Evil and Unlimited Power", *The Review of Metaphysics*, Vol. XX, 2, December, 1966, p. 288.

In Whitehead's thought there are three aspects of events which lay the grounds for the possibility of evil in the world. The first arises out of the self-creativity of the creature. Every actuality is, in a real sense, cause of itself; an element of freedom lies amongst the conditions of its becoming. Any actual entity, while in process, must take into account its past actual world and its ideal aim. The entity cannot change its past – that, it inherits – what it can modify is the initial aim provided by God. This is to say that there are limits to what can happen, but within those limits the entity actualizes itself in relative harmony or disharmony whith its world so that it emerges as a relatively positive or a relatively destructive force.

Secondly, the possibility for evil arises out of the necessity for contrast in nature. If God's aim toward valuation and order is to avoid triviality "society (must be) permissive of actualities with patterned intensity of feeling arising from adjusted contrasts."[25] What this means is that creative advance requires contrasting structures, but where particular contrasts fail to achieve satisfactory adjustments the character of things becomes mutually obstructive. The good of contrast lays the seed for the evil of opposition and conflict. The distuption which has its ontological possibility in the need for contrast is particulary heightened where we are dealing with creatures that have a relatively high degree of finite freedom. In that element of a contrast in existence belongs to the character of creativity itself, the elimination of all disharmony can be understood only as an eschatalogical symbol. On the other hand, where destructive incompatibility informs a situation, God's provided aim can only be "the best for that impasse. But if the best be bad, then the ruthlessness of God can be personified as Até – , the goddess of mischief. The chaff is burnt."[26]

The third aspect of things which gives rise to evil "lies in the fact that the past fades, that time is a 'perpetual perishing'."[27] Evil here achieves an ultimate quality : in this aspect, it simply belongs to the temporal character of events. Those occasions which we value, by their very nature, will perish in their subjective immediacy. You cannot grasp time "by the scruff of its neck."

Evil, then, is ontologically grounded; it lies there, as possibility,

[25] PR, p. 373-4.
[26] PR, p. 373.
[27] PR, p. 517.

with the freedom, valued contrast and temporality of being. Redemption, then, cannot mean the ultimate triumph over evil; such a triumph would entail the triumph over being as well. That is, evil cannot be eliminated as possibility from the world without eliminating the conditions of openness, significance and temporality which make life possible.

This means both that there are limits to the content of our redemptive faith, and that redemption must be re-defined to allow for new possibilities and new meanings. Redemption must be redemption in this (temporal and open) world, and not redemption from this world. Thus, we can agree with Ely that "religion demands that somehow evil shall not have the last word."[28] But we must interpret the meaning of this faith in two ways. First, it is a faith in the triumph over particular out-croppings of evil. There is no historically rooted evil that cannot be overcome, but the victory will be an historical victory, not an eternal one. There are no guarantees that certain disruptive social structures, or demonic conditions, though now overcome, will not reappear. And though there are undoubtedly limits to the possible extent of evil in the world, we do not know what those limits are. The truth is that there is no way of having our humanity apart from the experience of evil. We do not live without also suffering, and this is as true for the divine life as it is for ours. Secondly, the faith that evil shall not have the last word must be interpreted as affirming the value of life in the teeth of all that is destructive and demonic in life. The ultimate threat of evil is not the destruction of the physical life but the destruction of the finite will for life. Death is not through working out its evil when a life has been lost; its further work is the deprivation of the will to live in those who valued that now lost life. Thus, the desire for immortality must not be interpreted simply as the desire for prolonged personal existence; it must be seen as basically rooted in man's attempt to deal with the spiritually destructive effects of death upon those who still possess life. We cannot transcend death by reviving dead bodies or lost selves; this is the condition of our finite and temporal mode of existence. Nor do we transcend death through impassive indifference to loss of life – that way we simply lose our humanity. Rather, we transcend the destructive workings of death when we live with

[28] Ely, *The Religious Availability of Whitehead's God*, p. 37.

an intensity that accepts the pain and suffering in life in order to
live its beauty and purpose.

Our hope for a redeemed life, then, is inextricably tied up neither
with supernatural eschatological events in some distant future, nor
with the supernatural possibility for the eternal existence of disem-
bodied selves. Our redemptive hope lies in the faith that God has
the power to sustain our sense of the value and point of life, and
that God can bring us through those evils which threaten to drain
us of our will to live. What religion demands is not an ultimate
triumph of good or an ultimade realization of utopian aims; what
it demands is that nothing be able to overcome our feelings for the
value and goodness of live and that our "zest for existence be re-
freshed by the ever-present unfading importance of our immediate
actions."[29]

The redefination of redemptive faith has for its corollary a shift
in what religion demands "a theistic God should be." We can grant
that Whitehead's understanding of divine power takes account
of the modern concept of nature, but the crucial question remains
whether Whitehead has understood God's power so that it is relevant to the (redefined) requirements of a redemptive religion. In
Whitehead's thought, God's actions involve both poles of his being;
we must ask in what way these actions are redemptive.

All things aim at or feel their way towards being something definite
and towards achieving some satisfaction of unity and integration.
As the embodiment of the structure of possibility or definiteness,
God acts by being experienced as the lure for the creature's feelings,
where lure is understood as the dersuasive initiation of purpose and
guidance. The order of things upon which the world draws is informed by the givenness of the past, the possibility for the future
and the divine vision of the good. That is, part of the data to which
the creature responds is conditioned by the divine end of evoking
a response of maximum value out of each given situation. This is
a secular function of God, but it has its redemptive aspect insofar
as God functions here to provide the ground for the meaning of existence, and this in three ways, First, the integrity of God's aim
toward an increase in value provides a basis for a sense of purpose
and aim in life – sheer drift is avoided. Thus, what is a value-increa-
sing response from the divine perspective is a meaningful response

[29] PR, p. 533.

from the creature's perspective. Secondly, meaning in individual life requires its relevant participation in the good of the whole. God's vision of ideal possibilities for particular situations is always a vision which looks towards the abolishment of the antitheses between the general good and the particular interest. Thirdly, evil is rescued from sheer negation insofar as God's inexhaustible envisagement of relevant possibility suggests ways of transmuting present evil into some future good. In this view, God neither originates evil, nor undoes the evil of the past, but he does seek to draw some good outcome from it. God "uses what in the temporal world is mere wreckage."[30] We can summarize this by saying that God's concern for the increase in value is felt by the world as divine love.

In the concrete pole of his being, God receives, evaluates and preserves the activities of the world. He receives the world in his own way, purified and perfected by his integration vision of the whole. This "is the phase of perfected actuality, in which the many are one everlastingly, without the qualification of any loss either of individual identity or of completeness of unity."[31] The reception of the world in the being of God is redemptively transformative of the world. First ,God is the being who preserves the values of the past in their immediacy. In the divine life, there is effected"the transmutation of (each) temporal actuality into a living ever-present fact."[32] Thus, the perishing of the past, which is the ultimate evil of the earthly kingdom, finds its salvific repository in the " "heavenly kingdom" of God's being. Secondly, the disparate multiplicity of the world, its conflicts and oppositions, are transformed into an integrated experience in the divine life. What is obstructive and incongruous in the temporal world is ordered into its relation to the completed whole in God. Thirdly, what is done in the world receives its judgement as it passes into the immediacy of the divine life. What is sheer revolt, sheer destructiveness, sheer self-centeredness is judged as loss, and dismissed into everlasting rejection. The consequent nature of God functions to save what can be saved. - it is the "kingdom of heaven" – but what cannot be saved by transmutation is excluded from God's concrete and everlastingly transformative pole of being.

[30] PR, p. 525.
[31] PR, p. 532.
[32] PR, p. 531.

The transformation of the world into an everlasting reality in the life of God passes back into the world as part of the data to which the creature responds. Against the current talk about the "absence" of God, a Whiteheadian view stresses that God's way of having the world may enter significantly into the way in which the creature experiences both God and the world. Thus, Daniel Day Williams can write that "through the mutual immanence of all occasions, creatures have an experience, dimly, of God's consequent nature, as a felt unison of immediacy of the world without loss or obstruction. Here the wisdom which uses the wreckage in the temporal world, which saves everything which can be saved, and which passes in judgement upon the world is known directly. Thereby the creature's feeling is transformed through participation in the transformation which takes place initially in God."[33] We can say that the aspect of God that Williams is pointing to in Whitehead's thought is experienced by us as the merciful Father of the whole creation whose judgement is qualified by "a tenderness which loses nothing that can be saved."[34]

There is another way in which the consequent nature is experienced by the world. By reason of the reciprocal relation between God and the world, the love and suffering in the world passes into the immediacy of God's life where, purified by a wider sweep of interest, it floods back into the world. Suffering is transmuted by supplying its ideal counterparts and envisaging how it can contribute to a wider good; that is, God widens the perspective of our suffering into larger patterns where its contribution to a larger good can be envisaged. Whitehead reminds us that we must be careful not to disjoin the general good from individual interest or self-existence.

The sense of worth beyond itself is immediately enjoyed as an overpowering element in the individual self-attainment. It is in this way that the immediacy of sorrow and pain is transformed with an element of triumph. This is the notion of redemption through suffering which haunts the world.[35]

The dynamics of individuality and participation provide the ground that dialectically relates suffering to redemption. This, of course, does not constitute a "justification" of the suffering and travail

[33] Daniel D. Williams, "Deity, Monarchy & Metaphysics : Whitehead's Critique of the Theological Tradition", *The Relevance of Whitehead*, ed. 1. Leclerc, (New York : Macmillan, 1961), p. 367.

[34] PR, p. 525.

[35] PR, p. 531.

of the creation, but it does take us a step beyond saying that suffering is the way we have our humanity. Unless it be sheerly destructive, suffering need not be the last word. We can have a feeling for its wider good even as we know its present pain, and seek to live through it without being crippled by it.

Religious language expresses the immanence of the occasion of our suffering in God's being and God's transmutation of our suffering under the image of the suffering of incarnate deity. Thus we can say that suffering is the way God has his deity; that is, God's way of suffering is his deity, or we can reach metaphorically for a Christological image and say that God's suffering is his humanity. The soteriological intent of this statement is fundamentally the same as in the theological tradition. God's "humanity" means man's redemption; the reason for this is that God has His humanity or suffering in God's own way. That way is the way of transmutation; evil cannot overcome God but is transmuted by God, and that transmutation can be dimly felt by us. Whitehead summarizes this aspect of deity by calling God "the great companion, the fellow-sufferer who understands."[36]

There is another issue. It has to do with the limits of our hopes for a better future; what are the factors that we must consider in determining the extent of our hopes? The first factor concerns the mode of divine causality.

A causal relation exists where there "is the appropriation of some elements in the universe to be components the real internal constitution of its subject."[37] The mode of appropriation is through feeling – data are felt – and in this way they enter into the feeling subject as cause.[38] The medium, then, of the divine causality or activity is the creature's concrete taking hold in feeling of both the primordial order and the "consequential" responses of God to the world. This mode of divine communication is more akin to persuasive rather than coercive activity. Yet as Daniel Williams continually reminds us, there are coercive aspects in God's governance

---

[36] PR, p. 532.

[37] PR, p. 353.

[38] Whitehead employs the term "prehension" to refer to this basic way in which things experience or "feel" the world. Prehensions, then are feelings of data in such a way that the data organically inform the being of the prehender. In this way, the past becomes a component part of the present. Cf. PR, pp. 361-365.

of the world underlie our experience of God as persuasive.[39] No entity pursuing its own self-interest – which is the realization of some definite state of being – can fail to draw upon God as the the ultimate source of order and value. An entity can drastically modify God's causal influence, but to do so absolutely is to deprive itself of the possibility for actuality. Furthermore, the creature's failure to realize fully the aim that God holds before him is always the failure of an inadequate response to given circumstances. Opposition to God is opposition to the best possible outcome of a situation, so that when we oppose God, we stumble against the limits of our actions. The religious image for the consequences of ignoring or defying our creaturely boundaries is the wrath of God. Thus, God's activity (whether we label it secular or redemptive) may be felt by us as persuasive and not coercive, but our failure to take full account of that persuasion opens up the destructive elements in life, the "wrath of God." In this sense, God's redemptive activity is not without coercive force. The Whiteheadian concept of God does not leave us with a deity powerless in the face of those who thwart His ultimate purpose.

Secondly, we must, in concerning ourselves with the limits of our hopes, distinguish between universal, absolute redemption and redemption which is temporal, real and this worldly. A Whiteheadian perspective provides no assurance that every occasion of evil can be fully transmuted in a larger and wider good; sheer loss, tragic outcomes, pointless suffering are there as fact in the past and as possibility in the future; there is no getting behind these kind of events to some ultimate, justifying rationale. Creative goods certainly emerge out of past evils – so that creativity and not frustration is God's primary experience – but what is happening in the creative process is not that a past evil is being justified but that the present is being redeemed or freed from the evil of the past. In this sense the temporal character of things sets the limits to what we can hope for. Thus we cannot say that from some non-temporal perspective the evil in the world appears as a (long-run) good, though we can say that the evil that is now in our lives can and will be seen in a new light in God's temporal perspective. The point is that while

---

[39] Cf. Daniel Williams, "Deity, Monarchy & Metaphysics" in I. Leclerc, ed., *The Relevance of Whitehead*, and "How Does God Act" in W.L. Reese & E. Freeman, eds., *Process & Divinity*, (LaSalle, Ill. : Open Court Publishing Co., 1964).

a Whiteheadian perspective does not allow us (or God) to slough off the reality of evil, it so conceives the power of God and his relation to our life and history as to relegate evil to a less destructive and less dominating place in our psyche. Hope, or, more precisely, hope for a future of healing and value, can take the central place in our life attitude.

Redemption, then, involves both the quality of God's relation to us and the character of God's relation to history. To begin with, a redemptive faith is a faith that God is for us; the basis of this certainty in a Whiteheadian view is twofold. First, it lies in the assurance that supplies each new occasion with an aim for an ideal satisfaction. This means that there is a value seeking thrust in life which is a given in the universe and not something that man has to impose upon the nature things. It means that man is not forced back sheerly on his own resources to seek his way through the evils that confront him. It lies, also, in the assurance that whatever our feelings or actions, both those we are conscious of and those we are not, they are received by God with "the judgement of a tenderness which loses nothing that can be saved."[40] The reference here is to the particular occasions. In commenting upon the fact that the reception of one's feelings by another without rejection constitutes a basic factor in psychological therapy, Dr. Williams writes :

The communication of feeling to the other in the accepting situation constitutes a new standpoint in which the self may re-order and reinterpret its experience... When the feelings are received in "love" there is a transmutation which takes on the quality of the love which is given.[41]

This suggests that the category of feeling is an appropriate way of speaking about the mode of causality in the divine-human redemptive relationship. The use of such a category justifies our saying that we organically experience God's redemptive activity. Thus, we can stand assured, in faith, amidst our self-doubts, our destructive feelings, and our guilt, that God has the power to qualify these feelings, and that this qualification is a matter of "felt" perception rather than simply conceptual apprehension. We experience God's redemptive activity as the goodness of being; therefore we can say

---

[40] PR, p. 525.

[41] "How Does God Act" in Reese & Freeman, eds., *Process and Divinity*, pp. 176-177.

that the immanence in the world of God's specific feelings is the divine self-bestowal of goodness upon the world.

Secondly, redemption concerns God's relation to history. We can begin with Leslie Dewart's recommendation of the notion "of the radical openness of history – an openness which not even man's freedom can annihilate – as manifesting the true extent of the "word" that is possible with God."[42] This suggests the view that we are to look for God's redemptive power not in an eschatological foreclosure of history's moral ambiguity, but in an opening up of unlooked for historical possibilities. The point is that we need not accept the simple alternative that either God coercively moves history or history is cosmologically directionless. The view taken here is that history is always being lured toward higher and more harmonious ends; those ends may not reach immediate realization, but there is nothing that any creature can do to divest history of its teleological thrust. Conversely, the possibility held out to each individual to participate in the wider perspectives of history saves the individual from self-defeating and socially meaningless particularity.

The openness of the future to man is what allows for human freedom and creativity; the openness of the future to God constitutes the possibility of redemption. Augustine's response to the loss of his loved friend was to place his values outside history in the absolute and unchanging world of eternity. We no longer have that option. When we suffer loss we look, for hope, to the future. Our faith is not only that God did not require that loss, but that the openness of history leaves God free to elicit possibilities for our healing that are unimaginable to us

There is a moral side to historical openness that is germane to the meaning of redemption. It arises from the radical contingency of such a view,; namely, that there are no historical events or patterns of events that have to be, and that there is no worldly structure that is final. There hovers over history the possibility of the transcendence of its present limits, of the emergence of new values and of higher modes of being. Religion need not understand emergence as either the violation of the ultimate structure of possibility, nor as a unilateral act of God. Emergence is ontologically possible

[42] Leslie Dewart, *The Future of Belief*, (New York : Herder & Herder, 1966), p. 193.

because the present structure of things is rich with novel possibilities envisioned by God. It is precisely in this richness of possibility, in this range of responses held available to us, that the ground of our moral being lies. The measure of our morality is the quality of our history; we do not know what our moral limits are, though our history surely suggests that we are far from reaching its bounds.

The initiating aims supplied by God, then, and the self-creativity of the creature jointly constitute the ontological grounds for man's moral freedom. This means that the history of the world is replete with risk – for both God and the creature – but then there never was very much in our historical experience or our biblical heritage that would lead us to believe otherwise.

Finally, redemption involves our relation to our own existence. Were our moral sense, our will to live through suffering, our striving for achievement, simply swallowed up into the indifference of being then we would have to say that the very nature of things threatens our sanity with the emptiness of personal meaninglessness. Our sanity seems to depend upon life attaining some worth some lasting significance. Conversely, human sanity presupposes man's confidence or trust in the ultimate meaningfulness of his life.

It would be presumptuous for reflective thought to explain away man's sanity; the task is to account for it. We must begin then, with man's assumption of his ultimate worth; such a state of confidence must have its roots well below the cognitive level. Again Whitehead's category of feeling seems appropriate. When we ask what must be the nature of things that would lend intelligibility to this feeling confidence, we are moving into the area of the redemptive nature of God.

In a world lacking an everlasting being who preserves the values of that world, the creature's sense of self-worth is an illusion, all actions are ultimately uncovered as trivial passage. On the other hand, the mere affirmation of God does not provide the conceptual groud for creaturely significance. An absolute God, unaffected by human actions, empties that action of its significance. The significance of our actions for God requires that God be affected by them, that there be a genuine reciprocal relation between the divine life and ours. Significance here means making a difference. In order for our actions to make a difference in the quality of life, they must also make a difference in God's life. Thus, man's confidence in the ultimate worth of his particular existence requires, for its validity, a "consequent" pole of the divine being where God is immediately affected by the action of the world. In sum, the unfinished quality of God functions redemptively as that aspect of deity by virtue of which human activity achieves ontological value.

Here again, religion thrusts itself out toward the moral.[43] The moral quality of an act depends upon the seriousness of failure as well as the gains of accomplishement. The consequent pole of God's being means that the failure to achieve high aims, the harm we do to others either deliberately or through oversight, are not simply matters of private suffering. They affect God both in his reception of the emotional tone of the world and in the determination of the aim with which he responds to the world. "The initial aim is the best for that impasse. But if the best be bad, the ruthlessness of God can be personified as Até."[44] Thus, the doctrine of the effect of the world upon God accounts for the prophetic sense of awe before the moral act; it provides us with the link between the religious and the moral life.

What I want to argue finally is that Trinitarian theology is the historical expression of the church's redemptive faith. This point needs expansion.

God's redemptive activity is disclosed to man through concrete, historical happenings. Thus, it is by participation in an event or historic occasion in which insight into the character of things breaks through that we gain religious knowledge. Christian faith confesses that in the particular life Jesus of Nazareth, God's "word" was fully appropriated and responded to, so that it became available amongst men as the decisive expression of the eternal reality. The way in which the church chose to say how God and man were historically together in Jesus of Nazareth, and how transcendence and immanence are eternally together in deity, reflected in part the religious and philosophical thought of the Roman world. Underneath the Greek philosophical language of the Trinitarian dogma, however, lay the soteriological concern to accord full deity to the incarnate activity of God in order to sufficiently secure the faith in redemption through Jesus Christ. Trinitarian language then is redemptive language; what is ultimate in this redemptive language

---

[43] I am partially indebted here, to William Christian's unpublished paper "Whitehead's Theology" (mimeographed and distributed by the Society for Religion in Higher Education, 1967).

[44] PR, p. 373.

is the faith that God incarnate, fully present in the historic person of Jesus of Nazareth, is truly God and that there is no other God-transcendent to him. Thus, I agree with the modern Catholic formulation that

the Trinity of God's dealing with us is already the reality of God as he is in himself: 'tri-"personality." From that experience of our faith which the Word of God himself... gives, we can say that God's absolute self-communication to the world, as a mystery that has approached us, is in its ultimate originality called Father; as itself a principle acting in history, Son; as a gift bestowed on us and accepted, Holy Ghost.[45]

The God who gives himself to us, the God who acts in our history is the God who communicates himself absolutely to the world. When we know God "from that experience of our faith which the Word of God himself... gives," it is not as if there is another side of God to be known. Thus, Trinitarian language is not so much expressing ontological distinctions in deity as it is confessing that the whole of God's being is directed towards redemptive activity. It is affirming that the incarnate nature of the divine activity constitutes the redemptive (and therefore, creative) factor in the nature of things. We can link this up with our earlier discussion by saying that trinitarian language is the theological corollary to the "feeling of the value and purposeful direction of being.

As the expression of faith, trinitarian language lies midway between the faith itself and the metaphysic implied by the faith. This simply means that dogmatic theology is neither faith nor metaphysics. We all agree that dogma cannot live without faith; the argument here is that dogma cannot live without metaphysics. Surely theology must render trinitarian dogma intelligible by seeking for the ontology which underlies its expression of faith. At the same time, theology must exercise caution, and restrain itself from identifying, in any precise manner, ontological distinctions with the trinitarian ones.[46] God is complex in the way he has his being,

---

[45] Karl Rahner and Herbert Vorgirmler, *Theological Dictionary*, (New York : Herder and Herder, 1965), p. 472, approvingly quoted by Dewart, *The Future of Belief*, p. 148.

[46] For example, it would be tempting to correlate what the Catholic Theological Dictionary calls the ultimate originality of God with the primordial pole of God's being, and the "subjective" and "superjective" functions of the consequent pole (God's reception of the world, and the world's reception of God) with the Son and Holy Spirit. To say that Trinitarian theology was finally pointing to this

but we can hardly presume to garner a number for this complexity
out of the life of Jesus of Nazareth. This is not to say that there is
no legitimate basis for our use of the language Father, Son and
Holy Spirit, but it is to recognize that its legitimacy is historically
based, i.e., Christian trinitarian speech about God arose out of
the Hebrew and Greek heritage of Christian faith.

When we have said that, there is still more to say to justify trinitarian language. Throughout its history, the church has shunted
aside in its speech about God, the less personal terms such as source,
ground, logos, image, paraclete, etc... There is, perhaps, wisdom
in the church's insistence upon the personal language of Father,
Son, and Spirit as the most appropriate speech about God. Whitehead has said that religion is

an ultimate craving to infuse into the insistent particularity of emotion
that non-temporal generality which primarily belongs to conceptual thought
alone.[47]

There is, then, a line that cuts athwart theology and philosophy;
philosophical thought can never fully justify personal language
about God. What it can do is accept such language as part of the
data of the human experience of things. Augustine invented the
doctrine of appropriations to remind us that God is Father, Son,
and Holy Spirit. We have come full circle now; we may call God
Father, Son, and Holy Spirit to remind us that the ground of our
being is personal and that we experience him as for us.

---

kind of philosophic distinction is to forget the essentially religious meaning of
the dogma.

[47] PR, p. 23.

SELECTIVE BIBLIOGRAPHY

BOOKS

Aquinas, St. Thomas, *Commentary on the Metaphysics of Aristotle*. E.T., J. Rowan. Chicago: Henry Regnery Co., 1961.

—, *Concerning Being and Essence*. E.T., G. Leckie. New York: D. Appleton-Century, 1937.

—, On the Power of God. E.T., English Dominican Fathers. Westminster, Md.: Newman Press, 1952.

—, *Summa Contra Gentiles*. E.T., Anton Pegis. Vols. I-IV. Garden City, N.Y.: Doubleday, 1955-57.

—, *Summa Theologiae*. Thomas Gilby, O.P., General Editor. 60 volumes. New York: McGraw Hill; London: Eyre and Spottiswood, 1963-.

—, *Summa Theologica*. E.T., English Dominican Fathers. 22 volumes. London: Burns, Oates and Washburne Ltd., 1916-38.

—, *The Trinity and the Unicity of the Intellect*. E.T., Sister Brennan. St. Louis, Mo.: B. Herder, 1946.

—, *Truth*. E.T., R. Mulligan, J. McGlynn, and R. Schmidt. Chicago: H. Regnery and Co., 1952-54.

Athanasius, "De Incarnacion," in Edward Hardie, ed., *Christology of the Later Fathers*. (Vol. III of *The Library of Christian Classics*). Philadelphia: Westminister Press, 1954.

—, "Contra Arius," in *The Nicene and Post Nicene Fathers*. Second Series: Vol. IV. New York: Chas. Scribners, 1891.

Augustine, *The City of God*. E.T., Marcus Dods. New York: Modern Library, 1950.

—, *The Confessions of St. Augustine*. E.T., F.J. Sheed. London: Sheed and Ward, 1944.

—, "De Trinitate," in *The Nicene and Post Nicene Fathers*. First Series: Vol. III. New York: Chas. Scribners, 1887.

Barbour, Ian., *Issues in Science and Religion*. Englewood Cliffs, N.J.: Prentice Hall, 1966.

Basil, "Epistles," in *The Nicene and Post Nicene Fathers*. Second Series: Vol. VIII. New York: Chas. Scribners, 1893.

Battenhouse, Roy (ed.). A Companion to the Study of St. Augustine. New York: Oxford University Press, 1956.

Bergson, Henri, *Creative Evolution*. E.T., Arthur Mitchell. New York: Modern Library, 1944.

Biggs, C., *The Christian Platonists of Alexandria*. Oxford: Clarendon Press, 1913.

Brennan, Robert E. (ed.), *Essays in Thomism*. New York: Sheed and Ward, 1942.

Brightman, E.S., *A Philosophy of Religion*. New York: Prentice Hall, 1950.

—, *Problem of God*. New York: Abingdon Press, 1930.

Burnaby, J., *Amor Dei*; *A Study of the Religion of St. Augustine*. London: Hodder and Stoughton, 1930.

Cherniss, H.F., *The Platonism of Gregory of Nyssa*. Berkeley: University of California Press, 1930.

Chesterton, G.K., *St. Thomas Aquinas*. London: Sheed and Ward, 1933.

Christian, William, *An Interpretation of Whitehead's Metaphysics*. New Haven: Yale University Press, 1959.

Cobb, John, *A Christian Natural Theology*. Philadelphia: Westminister Press, 1965.

Cochran, C.N., *Christianity and Classical Culture*. New York: Oxford University Press, 1957.

Copleston, F., *Aquinas*. Baltimore: Penguin Books, 1961.

—, *A History of Philosophy*. Vol. II: *Augustine to Scotus*. London: Burns, Oates and Washbourne, 1950.

Danielou, J., *Origen*. E.T., W. Mitchell. New York: Sheed and Ward, 1955.

D'Arcy, M.C. (ed.), *A Monument to St. Augustine*. New York: Meridian Books, 1961.

—, *The Pain of this World and the Providence of God*. London: Longmans, Green, 1953.

—, *Thomas Aquinas*. London: Ernest Benn, 1930.

Das, R., *The Philosophy of Whitehead*. London, James Clark and Co., 1937.

Dewart, Leslie, *The Future of Belief*. New York: Herder and Herder, 1966.

Elmore, J., *The Theology of the Suffering God in Berdyaev, Hartshorne and Reinhold Niebuhr*. Unpublished PhD thesis, Columbia University, 1963.

Ely, Stephen, *The Religious Availability of Whitehead's God*. Madison: University of Wisconsin Press, 1942.

Emmet, D., *The Nature of Metaphysical Thinking*. London: Macmillan, 1949.

—, *Whitehead's Philosophy of Organism*. London: Macmillan, 1932.

Foley, Leo A., *A Critique of the Philosophy of Being of A.N. Whitehead in the Light of Thomistic Philosophy*. Washington D.C.: Catholic University Press, 1946.

Foss, Martin, *The Idea of Perfection*. Princeton: Princeton University Press, 1946.

Garrigou-Lagrange, R., *Christian Reflection and Contemplation*. E.T., Sister Doyle. St. Louis: Herder, 1939.

—, *God: His Existence and His Nature*. 2 vols. E.T., Dom Bede Rose. St. Louis: B. Herder, 1934-36.

—, *The One God*. E.T., Dom Bede Rose. St. Louis: Herder, 1943.

—, *The Trinity and God the Creator*. E.T., L. Eckhoff. St. Louis: Herder, 1952.

Gilson, E., *The Christian Philosophy of St. Augustine*. E.T., L.E. M. Lynch. New York: Random House, 1960.

—, *The Christian Philosophy of St. Thomas Aquinas*. E.T., L.K. Shool. New York: Sheed and Ward, 1939.

—, *God and Philosophy*. New Haven: Yale University Press, 1941.

—, *The History of Christian Philosophy in the Middle Ages*. New York: Random House, 1955.

—, *Reason and Revelation in the Middle Ages*. New York: Chas. Scribners, 1939.

—, *The Spirit of Medieval Philosophy.* E.T., A.C. Downes. New York: Chas. Scribners, 1940.

—, *The Spirit of Thomism.* New York: P.J. Kennedy, 1964.

Gregory of Nazianzen, "The Theological Orations" in Edward Hardie, ed. *Christology of the Later Fathers* (Vol. III of the Library of Christian Classics). Philadelphia, Westminister Press, 1954.

Gregory of Nyssa, "On Not Three Gods," in Edward Hardie, ed., *Christology of the Later Fathers,* (Vol. III of The Library of Christian Classics). Philadelphia, Westminster Press, 1954.

Hammerschmidt, W., *Whitehead's Philosophy of Time.* New York: Kings Crown Press, 1952.

Hartshorne, Charles, *Beyond Humanism: Essays in the New Philosophy of Nature.* Chicago: Willett, Clark and Co., 1937.

—, *The Divine Relativity:* A Social Conception of God. The Terry Lectures, 1947. New Haven: Yale University Press, 1948.

—, *The Logic of Perfection.* LaSalle, Ill.: The Open Court Publishing Co., 1962.

—, *Man's Vision of God and the Logic of Theism.* Chicago: Willett, Clark and Co., 1941.

—, *Philosophers Speak of God.* (With William L. Reese). Chicago: The University of Chicago Press, 1953.

—, *Reality as Social Process: Studies in Metaphysics and Religion.* Glencoe: The Free Press and Boston: The Beacon Press, 1950.

Hartshorne, Marion Holmes, *The Significance of Classical and Relativistic Mechanics for the Cosmological Argument.* Unpublished thesis, Union Theological Seminary, 1938.

Hatch, E., *The Influence of Greek Ideas on Christianity.* New York: Harper, 1957.

Hodgson, Leonard, *The Doctrine of the Trinity.* New York: Chas. Scribners, 1944.

Johnson, A.H., *Whitehead's Theory of Reality.* New York: Dover, 1962.

Kelly, J.N.D., *The Athanasian Creed.* New York: Harper, 1964.

—, *Early Christian Creeds.* London: Longmans, Green, 1950.

—, *Early Christian Doctrines.* New York: Harper, 1959.

Klein, F., *The Doctrine of the Trinity.* E.T., Daniel Sullivan. New York: P.J. Kenedy & Sons, 1940.

Kline, G. (ed.), *Alfred North Whitehead: Essays on His Philosophy.* Englewood Cliffs, New York: Prentice Hall, 1963.

Lawrence, Nathaniel, *Whitehead's Philosophical Development.* Berkeley: University of California Press, 1956.

Leclerc, I. (ed.), *The Relevance of Whitehead.* New York: Macmillan, 1961.

—, *Whitehead's Metaphysics.* New York: The Humanities Press, 1965.

Loomer, Bernard, *The Theological Significance of the Method of Empirical Analysis on the Philosophy of Alfred North Mhitehead.* Chicago: University of Chicago Press, 1945.

Lovejoy, A., *The Great Chain of Being.* Cambridge, Mass.: Harvard University Press, 1936.

Maritain, J., *The Angelic Doctor.* The Life and Thought of St. Thomas Aquinas. E.T., J.G. Scanlan. London: Sheed and Ward, 1931.

—, *Bergsonian Philosophy and Thomism.* E.T., M. Andison, New York: Philosophical Library, 1955.

—, *The Degrees of Knowledge*. E.T., B. Wall and M. Adamson. London: Bles, 1937.

—, *St. Thomas and the Problem of Evil*. Milwaukee: Marquette University Press, 1942.

—, *St. Thomas Aquinas, Angel of the Schools*. London, 3rd ed., 1946.

Mascall, E.L., *He Who Is*. A Study in Traditional Theism. Longmans, Green, 1943.

Meland, B., *Faith and Culture*. New York: Oxford University Press, 1953.

—, *The Realities of Faith*. New York: Oxford University Press, 1962.

Ogden, S., *The Reality of God*. New York: Harper, 1966.

Origen, *Contra Celsum*. E.T., Henry Chadwick. Cambridge: Cambridge University Press, 1953.

—, De Principiis. E.T., G.W. Butterworth. London: SPCK, 1936.

Pohle, J. and Preuss, A., *The Divine Trinity*. St. Louis, Mo.: Herder, 1930.

—, *God, the Author of Nature and the Supernatural*. St. Louis: Herder, 1934.

Patterson, Robert, *The Concept of God in the Philosophy of St. Thomas Aquinas*. London: Allen, 1933.

Pittenger, W.N., *The Word Incarnate*. New York: Harper & Bros., 1959.

Prestige, G.L., *Fathers and Heretics*. New York: Macmillan, 1940.

—, *God in Patristic Thought*. London: SPCK, 1952.

Preston, R., *Causality and the Thomistic Theory of Knowledge*. Washington, D.C.: Catholic University of America, 1960.

Pringle-Pattison, A.S., *The Idea of God in Recent Philosophy*. New York: Oxford University Press, 1920.

Rahner, Karl, *Theological Investigations*. Vol. I. E.T., C. Ernst. Baltimore: Helicon Press, 1961.

Rawlinson, A.E.J. (ed.), *Essays on the Trinity and Incarnation*. London: Longmans, Green, 1928.

Reese, W.L. and Freeman, E. (eds.), *Process and Divinity*. La Salle, Ill.: Open Court Publishing Co., 1964.

Richardson, Cyril, *The Doctrine of Trinity*. Nashville, Tenn.: Abingdon, 1958.

Schilpp, Paul Arthur (ed.), *The Philosophy of Alfred North Whitehead*. New York: The Tudor Publishing Co., 1951.

Sertillanges, A.D., *Foundations of Thomistic Philosophy*. E.T., G. Anstruther. London: Sands, 1931.

—, *St. Thomas Aquinas and his Work*. E.T., G. Anstruther. London: Burns Oates, 1933.

Tillich, Paul, *Systematic Theology*. 3 Vols. Chicago: University of Chicago Press, 1951-63.

Tolley, W.P., *The Idea of God in the Philosophy of St. Augustine*. New York: R.R. Smith Inc., 1930.

Tresmontant, Claude, *Toward the Knowledge of God*. E.T., R. Olsen. Baltimore: Helicon Press, 1961.

Welch, Claude, *In This Name*. New York: Chas. Scribners, 1952.

Whitehead, A.N., *Adventures of Ideas*. New York: Macmillan, 1933.

—, *The Concept of Nature*. Cambridge: Cambridge University Press, 1920.

—, *Essays in Science and Philosophy*. New York: Philosophical Library, 1947.

—, *The Function of Reason*. Princeton: Princeton University Press, 1929.

—, *Modes of Thought*. New York: Macmillan, 1938.

—, *Process and Reality.* New York: Macmillan, 1929.

—, *Religion in the Making.* New York: Macmillan, 1926.

—, *Science and the Modern World.* New York: Macmillan, 1925.

—, *Symbolism, its Meaning and Effect.* New York: Macmillan, 1927.

Williams, Daniel Day, *God's Grace and Man's Hope.* New York: Harpers, 1949.

—, *The Spirit and the Forms of Love.* New York: Harper & Row, 1968.

Wolfson, H., *The Philosophy of the Church Fathers.* 2nd ed. revised. Cambridge: Harvard University Press, 1964.